The

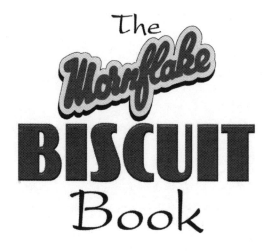

BISCUIT
Book

foulsham
LONDON • NEW YORK • TORONTO • SYDNEY

foulsham

The Publishing House, Bennetts Close, Cippenham,
Slough, Berkshire, SL1 5AP, England

ISBN 0-572-02980-2

A CIP record for this book is available from the British Library.

Printed in Great Britain by Cox & Wyman Ltd, Reading, Berkshire

Contents

Introduction   4

Mornflake – Milling Oats Since 1675   5

Where Do Oats Come From?   6

How We Make Mornflake Oats   9

Notes on the Recipes   11

Crisp and Crunchy Biscuits   12

Moist and Crumbly Bites   26

Iced and Sandwich Biscuits   36

Melt-in-the-Mouth Biscuits   49

Soft and Chewy Biscuits   60

Bumper Breakfast Bars   67

Savoury Specials   75

No-bake Cookies   84

Index   94

Introduction

There is nothing as tempting as the aroma of freshly baked biscuits. Plus, they are so therapeutic to make because not only are they fun and easy to prepare but also it is so satisfying to survey a pile of golden discs or chocolatey squares cooling on a wire rack in your own kitchen. The only thing to top it is the pleasure of eating them!

Bought biscuits can be full of hidden additives, but if you bake your own you can be sure you are using only good, wholesome ingredients and that they are a great source of energy and fibre.

We now know there are two types of dietary fibre – soluble and insoluble. Bran is insoluble and is important for helping to keep your digestion running freely, but it should always be eaten with soluble fibre – like oats, other grains and dried fruits. Oats are also important for helping to reduce your LDL cholesterol, and what better way of eating them than in scrumptious biscuits?

This book is packed with wonderfully easy recipes for every sort of biscuit you could possibly wish to make – from chewy cereal bars packed with the goodness of oats, bran, honey, dried fruit and nuts to traditional favourites like custard creams.

Milling Oats Since 1675

Not many companies today can trace their history back to 325 years before the current millennium began, but Mornflake can, having first milled oats for local farmers in the beautiful Cheshire countryside in 1675!

Today, 14 generations later, the company continues to be independently owned and managed by the direct descendants of those millers. With expertise and skills handed down from fathers to sons, this unparalleled experience ensures that you can continue to enjoy oat products of the highest possible quality from Mornflake.

Mornflake's milling process carefully retains the whole oat grain containing both germ and bran, removing only the inedible outer husk. Modern technology at this 'state-of-the-art' mill is so sophisticated that the grain can be precisely sorted for shape, size and moisture so it is optimised for each of the many types of oat product, from rolled oats to oatmeals and oat flours. No wonder Mornflake oats regularly win the European milling industry's top International Gold Medals for quality, purity and consistency.

Where Do Oats Come From?

You might think that breakfast cereals were a product of the late twentieth century. Not true! Archaeologists have found evidence that the Ancient Greeks and Romans enjoyed tucking into a bowl of porridge. Because oats are a hardy crop, able to survive extreme cold, they were eaten by tribes throughout northern Europe. When oats reached Scotland they were known as 'pilcorn' and soon became part of the daily fare. Today they remain as popular as ever and David Henderson from Montrose in Scotland – who died in 1998 at the age of 109 and is the longest-living Briton on record – attributed his age and good health to hard work and a daily bowl of porridge.

Throughout the Middle Ages, oatmeal cakes and cheese were the monotonous staple of the British peasant's diet. In the seventeenth and eighteenth centuries, oats gradually replaced barley and rye because they grew better, but eventually the rapid developments in agriculture resulted in a decline in oat production as it was replaced by wheat.

The revival of oats came with the famous American doctor, John Kellogg. Although he is best known for inventing Cornflakes in 1899, he also created 'granola', an oat-based cereal, in the 1860s. Together with Shredded Wheat and Weetabix – the only cereal invented in England – these cereals were sold as health foods. At the beginning of the nineteenth century, a Swiss nutritionist, Dr Bircher, adapted the old Swiss custom of mixing porridge oats with fresh or dried fruit to create muesli (a German word meaning 'mixture'). He gave it to patients at his health clinic in Zurich and it soon became popular all over Europe. Gradually oats became fashionable again.

Today, oats are grown in almost every part of the world but the most important areas of production are North America, Scandinavia, Russia, Great Britain and Australia.

Types of oats

Oats are an extremely versatile cereal and are available from Mornflake in many grades for breakfasts and cooking.

Rolled or flaked oats

These are given many different names – flaked oats, oat flakes, quick oats, easy oats and porridge oats are some of the more common – but are basically the same type of product. Mornflake produces them under the name Superfast Oats. They are partially cooked during the milling process and are ideal for making porridge, muesli, parkin and flapjack biscuits.

Jumbo oats

These are the largest variety of flaked oats and are best for making a good, thick porridge with a more pronounced texture. They have a slightly nutty flavour and make superb biscuits.

Mornflake organic oats

Organic oats are made from oats especially grown to the established organic standards laid down by the UK Register of Organic Food Standards, which means the crops rely for their purity on the goodness of the soil, enriched only by natural means.

Every oat crop under contract for Mornflake Organic Oats is grown to strict standards by farmers who use traditional farming methods without any chemical fertilisers.

Oatmeal

Medium oatmeal is made from ground wholegrain oats and has a pleasant, slightly rough texture, ideal for porridge, oatcakes and parkin. Medium oatmeal is the best variety for coating fish and meat before frying and is good in stuffings and crumble toppings. Fine oatmeal makes a lovely, smooth milk pudding. This is the type to use as a thickening agent for soups, sauces and gravy.

Coarse oatmeal is similar to medium oatmeal but, as its name suggests, it is ground to a coarser grade for extra texture.

Pinhead oatmeal can be made into delicious traditional Scottish porage, which is more granular than the porridge most people are used to. Pinhead oatmeal is the chunkiest grade of oatmeal in general usage and can be ideal for adding texture as well as nutritional value to soups, stews and toppings for pies and puddings.

Oat bran

Oat bran is milled from the two thin layers that are found beneath the outer husk or 'hull' of the oat grain. These layers are particularly rich in soluble fibre. Oat bran makes a very smooth porridge and can be sprinkled into many recipes, including cereals and salad dishes, or used in baking for higher-fibre food.

Oat flour

Oat flour is very fine, smooth-textured flour. Ideal as a baby food, it also makes a good thickening agent. Mixed with wheat flour, it is delicious in biscuits, bread, cakes, scones and pastry (paste).

Making oat flour

Oat flour is not as readily available in supermarkets as other products, but it is easy to make your own. Simply place some Mornflake oats or fine or medium Mornflake oatmeal in a liquidiser or food processor and grind to flour. Keep a jar ready made up to add oat power to your cooking.

How We Make Mornflake Oats

The miller has to obtain from the oat the kernel from which oatmeal and porridge oats are made and, to do this, a variety of machines and different processes are used.

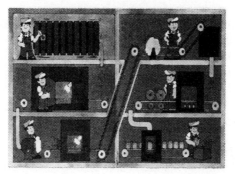

1 Cleaning

When oats arrive at the mill they contain all sorts of impurities – ranging from seeds to much larger substances such as iron, coal, straw, sticks and stones. All this extraneous matter has to be removed from the grain while it is still in its whole state. This is accomplished by the use of many ingenious machines that take advantage of the differences in size, shape, specific gravity and colour of the grain and the impurities. This is done by sieves, currents of air (which we call aspirators) and by indented cylinders or discs that pick up the smaller grain or seeds and leave the larger grain, which passes on to the next stage.

2 Roasting or kilning

The oat passes through a machine that blows hot air from a furnace over it and dries the grain down from its natural moisture content of 16 per cent to approximately 6 per cent. It is then cooled and stored (or conditioned, as we call it), until it is required for the next process.

3 Shelling or removal of husk

The oats are shelled by passing through a machine that throws them at a very high speed against a stationary rubber surface. This has the effect of springing the kernel, or groat, from the shell before the whole mass passes over an aspirator, which is able to blow away the oat husk because of its lighter density. This enables the miller to separate the husk and to grind it directly into cattle feed, while the groat passes on to the next stage.

4 Polishing, cutting, grading and cleaning

The groat now passes through polishers and over a table separator, which extracts any unshelled oats and returns them to the shelling process. The groat is cut on rotary granulators, each groat being cut into three pieces. It is then graded on rotary sieves and aspirated to blow away any remaining small pieces of oat husk. From this point on the meal is called pinhead oatmeal, and this is stored until it is required for cooking into porridge oats.

5 Cooking, flaking and drying

The pinhead oatmeal is passed over a cooker where it is cooked with high-temperature steam. This partial cooking reduces the time needed when you come to make porridge in your home. After cooking, the pinhead oatmeal is flaked on a flaking roll, then dried on a drying band and cooled.

6 Packing

Automatic packing machines are used to pack Mornflake oats into cartons and visi-pillow packs. Machines fill these packs by weight, and these are then placed in corrugated fibreboard cases for delivery to the shops ready for you to buy and enjoy.

Notes on the Recipes

- All ingredients are given in imperial, metric and American measures. Follow one set only in a recipe.

- American terms are given in brackets.

- All spoon measures are level: 1 tsp = 5 ml; 1 tbsp = 15 ml.

- Eggs are medium unless otherwise stated.

- Ingredients are listed in the order you use them.

- All cooking times are approximate. Ovens do vary, so use them as a guide only. Fan ovens do not need preheating.

- Always cook on the shelf just above the centre of the oven unless otherwise stated. If using two baking (cookie) sheets, put one in the centre and the other just above.

- Check biscuits during cooking and if browning unevenly, turn the baking sheets or tins (pans) around.

- I have called for butter only in some recipes because the flavour is important. You could use a butter-flavoured spread instead in recipes that call for softened butter. If you use a reduced-fat variety in place of ordinary butter or margarine, make sure it is suitable for baking.

Crisp and Crunchy Biscuits

Probably the epitome of biscuits – those that snap as you break them, crunch as you bite them and munch as you chew them up! These are the best types for dunking in your tea or coffee; because they are crisp, they hold the moisture just long enough to get them from cup to mouth!

Sunflower Vanilla Cookies

Makes about 20

100 g/4 oz/½ cup butter or margarine, plus extra for greasing
100 g/4 oz/½ cup demerara sugar
15 ml/1 tbsp clear honey
5 ml/1 tsp vanilla essence (extract)
100 g/4 oz/1 cup Superfast Oats
50 g/2 oz/½ cup wholemeal flour
50 g/2 oz/½ cup plain (all-purpose) flour
10 ml/2 tsp baking powder
50 g/2 oz/½ cup sunflower seeds
About 15 ml/1 tbsp milk

1   Put the butter or margarine in a saucepan with the sugar and honey. Heat gently, stirring occasionally, until melted. Remove from the heat and add the vanilla essence.

2   Mix the oats with the two flours and the baking powder. Stir into the melted mixture with the sunflower seeds. Beat thoroughly with a wooden spoon, adding enough of the milk to form a firm dough.

3   Grease two baking (cookie) sheets. Shape the mixture into walnut-sized balls and place well apart on the sheets. Flatten slightly.

4   Bake one above the other in a preheated oven at 190°C/375°F/gas 5/fan oven 170°C for about 20 minutes until richly golden, swapping the sheets over half way through cooking.

5   Remove from the oven and allow to cool slightly, then transfer to a wire rack to cool completely. Store in an airtight container.

Double Chocolate Crisps

Makes about 20

100 g/4 oz/½ cup butter or margarine, plus extra for greasing
100 g/4 oz/½ cup granulated sugar
15 ml/1 tbsp golden (light corn) syrup
85 g/3½ oz/scant 1 cup self-raising (self-rising) flour
15 g/½ oz/2 tbsp cocoa (unsweetened chocolate) powder
2.5 ml/½ tsp bicarbonate of soda (baking soda)
100 g/4 oz/1 cup Superfast Oats
150 g/5 oz/1¼ cups plain (semi-sweet) cooking chocolate

1 Put the butter or margarine in a saucepan with the granulated sugar and syrup and heat gently, stirring occasionally, until melted.

2 Sift the flour, cocoa and bicarbonate of soda together and stir in the oats.

3 Remove the melted mixture from the heat and stir in the oat mixture. Beat with a wooden spoon until thoroughly blended. Cool slightly.

4 Lightly grease two baking (cookie) sheets. Shape the mixture into walnut-sized balls and place well apart on the sheets. Flatten slightly.

5 Bake one above the other in a preheated oven at 180°C/350°F/gas 4/fan oven 160°C for 15 minutes, swapping the sheets over half way through cooking.

6 Remove from the oven and allow to cool for 5 minutes, then transfer to a wire rack to cool completely.

7 Break up the chocolate and place it in a bowl over a pan of hot water. Stir until melted. Alternatively, melt the chocolate briefly in the microwave.

8   Spread the underside of each biscuit with chocolate and leave to set chocolate-side up. Store in an airtight container.

Oat Thins

Makes about 16

100 g/4 oz/1 cup Superfast Oats
50 g/2 oz/½ cup self-raising (self-rising) flour
50 g/2 oz/¼ cup caster (superfine) sugar
1.5 ml/¼ tsp salt
50 g/2 oz/¼ cup butter or margarine, cut into small pieces, plus extra for greasing
About 30 ml/2 tbsp milk

1   Mix the dry ingredients together in a bowl.
2   Add the butter or margarine and rub in using the fingertips.
3   Mix with enough of the milk to form a firm dough.
4   Knead gently on a lightly floured surface. Roll out thinly and cut into rounds using a 7.5 cm/3 in cutter, re-kneading and rolling the trimmings as necessary.
5   Grease two baking (cookie) sheets. Arrange the biscuits on the sheets and bake one above the other in a preheated oven at 180°C/350°F/ gas 4/fan oven 160°C for about 15–20 minutes until golden brown, swapping the sheets over half way through cooking.
6   Remove from the oven and allow to cool slightly, then transfer to a wire rack to cool completely. Store in an airtight container.

Butter Oat Fingers

Makes 12

75 g/3 oz/¹/₃ cup butter, softened, plus extra for greasing
75 g/3 oz/¹/₃ cup demerara sugar
100 g/4 oz/1 cup Superfast Oats

1 Grease an 18 cm/7 in square shallow baking tin (pan).
2 Beat the butter and sugar together until light and fluffy. Mix in the oats.
3 Press into the tin.
4 Bake in a preheated oven at 220°C/425°F/gas 7/fan oven 200°C for 15–20 minutes until evenly golden brown.
5 Remove from the oven and allow to cool slightly, then mark into 12 fingers and loosen round the edge. When almost cold, cut into fingers and transfer to a wire rack to cool completely. Store in an airtight container.

Almond Tuiles

Makes 18

75 g/3 oz/¹/₃ cup unsalted (sweet) butter
75 g/3 oz/¹/₃ cup caster (superfine) sugar
50 g/2 oz/¹/₂ cup plain (all-purpose) flour
75 g/3 oz/³/₄ cup flaked (slivered) almonds

1 Beat the butter and sugar together until light and fluffy.
2 Work in the flour and almonds.
3 Line a baking (cookie) sheet with non-stick baking parchment. Put nine heaped teaspoonfuls of the mixture on the sheet and flatten with a wet palette knife.

4   Bake in a preheated oven at 200°C/400°F/gas 6/fan oven 180°C for about 7 minutes until lightly golden.

5   Remove from the oven and transfer to a wire rack to cool. Repeat with the rest of the mixture. Store in an airtight container.

Cornish Fairings

Makes 20

100 g/4 oz/½ cup butter or margarine, plus extra for greasing
100 g/4 oz/½ cup light brown sugar
15 ml/1 tbsp clear honey
175 g/6 oz/1½ cups plain (all-purpose) flour
5 ml/1 tsp bicarbonate of soda (baking soda)
2.5 ml/½ tsp mixed (apple-pie) spice
2.5 ml/½ tsp ground cinnamon
2.5 ml/½ tsp ground ginger

1   Put the butter or margarine, sugar and honey in a saucepan and heat gently, stirring occasionally, until melted. Remove from the heat.

2   Sift the flour, bicarbonate of soda and the spices together. Stir into the melted mixture and beat well with a wooden spoon.

3   Grease two baking (cookie) sheets. Shape the mixture into 20 small balls and place them well apart on the sheets.

4   Bake one above the other in a preheated oven at 180°C/ 350°F/gas 4/fan oven 160°C for 13–15 minutes, swapping the sheets over half way through cooking, until a deep golden brown and cracking slightly on top.

5   Remove from the oven and allow to cool slightly, then transfer to a wire rack to cool completely. Store in an airtight container.

Oat Crunchies

These are crunchy but they do have a tendency to be slightly chewy in the centre – especially if you don't flatten them enough!

Makes about 20

100 g/4 oz/½ cup butter or margarine, plus extra for greasing
100 g/4 oz/½ cup light brown sugar
15 ml/1 tbsp golden (light corn) syrup
100 g/4 oz/1 cup self-raising (self-rising) flour
100 g/4 oz/1 cup Superfast Oats
2.5 ml/½ tsp bicarbonate of soda (baking soda)

1 Put the butter or margarine, sugar and syrup in a saucepan and heat gently, stirring occasionally, until melted.

2 Mix together the remaining ingredients. Remove the melted mixture from the heat and stir in the flour mixture with a wooden spoon. Beat well until thoroughly blended.

3 Lightly grease two baking (cookie) sheets. Shape the mixture into walnut-sized balls and place well apart on the sheets. Flatten with the palm of your hand or a palette knife.

4 Bake one above the other in a preheated oven at 180°C/350°F/gas 4/fan oven 160°C for about 15 minutes until a rich golden brown, swapping the sheets over half way through cooking.

5 Remove from the oven and allow to cool for 5 minutes, then transfer to a wire rack to cool completely. Store in an airtight container.

Brandy Snaps

You can fill these with whipped cream, if liked, before serving.

Makes 12

75 g/3 oz/⅓ cup butter, plus extra for greasing
75 g/3 oz/⅓ cup caster (superfine) sugar
45 ml/3 tbsp golden (light corn) syrup
65 g/2½ oz/scant ¾ cup plain (all-purpose) flour
15 g/½ oz/2 tbsp wheat or oat bran
5 ml/1 tsp ground ginger
10 ml/2 tsp brandy

1 Put the butter, sugar and syrup in a saucepan and heat gently until melted, stirring occasionally. Stir in the flour, bran, ginger and brandy.

2 Line a baking (cookie) sheet with non-stick baking parchment. Using a quarter of the mixture, drop 3 spoonfuls of the mixture well apart on the sheet.

3 Bake in a preheated oven at 180°C/350°F/gas 4/fan oven 160°C for about 9 minutes or until deep golden, well spread out and full of bubbly holes. Remove from the oven.

4 Grease the handle of a wooden spoon. Lift one brandy snap off the baking sheet with a fish slice and quickly mould round the handle. Let it set briefly, then slide off and transfer to a wire rack. Mould the others in the same way. If they become hard before you mould them, pop them back in the oven briefly to soften again. Cook and mould the remaining mixture.

5 When cold, store in an airtight container.

Biscotti

These are traditionally made with almonds (which you can, of course, use instead, in which case use almond essence instead of vanilla) but this hazelnut version has a delicious mellow, sweet nuttiness.

Makes about 24

100 g/4 oz/1 cup whole unblanched hazelnuts (filberts)
100 g/4 oz/1 cup plain (all-purpose) flour
50 g/2 oz/¼ cup caster (superfine) sugar
A pinch of salt
1.5 ml/¼ tsp bicarbonate of soda (baking soda)
A few drops of vanilla essence (extract)
1 large egg, separated
Butter or margarine for greasing

1 Spread out the nuts on a baking (cookie) sheet. Bake in a preheated oven at 180°C/350°F/gas 4/fan oven 160°C for about 15 minutes until toasted but not burnt.

2 Grind half the nuts in a blender or food processor and very roughly chop the remainder, leaving the pieces quite large.

3 Tip the ground nuts into a bowl and stir in the flour, sugar, salt, bicarbonate of soda and vanilla.

4 Lightly beat the egg white. Add the egg yolk to the flour mixture and mix in, adding enough of the white to form a firm dough. Tip out on to a surface and work in the chopped nuts.

5 Shape the dough into 2 rolls about 2.5 cm/1 in diameter.

6 Grease a baking (cookie) sheet and put the rolls on the sheet. Bake in the preheated oven for 15 minutes.

7 Remove from the oven and allow the rolls to cool slightly. Using a sharp knife, cut each one diagonally into 1 cm/½ in thick slices. Return to the baking sheet and bake for a further 30 minutes until crisp and golden.

8 Remove from the oven and transfer to a wire rack to cool completely. Store in an airtight container.

Coconut Oat Cookies

Makes 18

65 g/2½ oz/generous ½ cup Superfast Oats
40 g/1½ oz/⅓ cup plain (all-purpose) flour
75 g/3 oz/⅓ cup caster (superfine) sugar
A pinch of salt
40 g/1½ oz/⅓ cup desiccated (shredded) coconut
75 g/3 oz/⅓ cup butter or margarine
2.5 ml/½ tsp vanilla essence (extract)
1 egg white, lightly beaten

1 Mix the oats, flour, sugar, salt and coconut together in a bowl.

2 Melt the butter or margarine with the vanilla essence. Add to the oat mixture with the egg white and mix until thoroughly blended.

3 Line two baking (cookie) sheets with non-stick baking parchment. Put nine heaped dessertspoonfuls of the mixture well apart on each of the sheets. Bake one above the other in a preheated oven at 180°C/350°F/gas 4/fan oven 160°C for about 15 minutes until golden brown, swapping the sheets over half way through cooking.

4 Remove from the oven and allow to cool slightly, then transfer to a wire rack to cool completely. Store in an airtight container.

Black and White Florentines

Makes about 12

65 g/2½ oz/generous ¼ cup butter
50 g/2 oz/¼ cup caster (superfine) sugar
15 g/½ oz/1½ tbsp chopped mixed (candied) peel
25 g/1 oz/2 tbsp glacé (candied) cherries, roughly chopped
25 g/1 oz angelica, chopped
25 g/1 oz/3 tbsp sultanas (golden raisins)
40 g/1½ oz/⅓ cup flaked (slivered) almonds, roughly chopped
15 g/½ oz/2 tbsp plain (all-purpose) flour
75 g/3 oz/¾ cup plain (semi-sweet) chocolate
75 g/3 oz/¾ cup white chocolate

1 Put the butter and sugar in a saucepan and heat gently, stirring occasionally, until melted. Bring to the boil.

2 Remove from the heat and stir in all the remaining ingredients except the two types of chocolate.

3 Line two baking (cookie) sheets with non-stick baking parchment. Drop heaped teaspoonfuls of the mixture well apart on the sheets. Bake one above the other in a preheated oven at 180°C/350°F/gas 4/fan oven 160°C for about 10 minutes, swapping the sheets over half way through cooking, until the Florentines are a rich golden brown.

4 Remove from the oven and allow to cool for 5 minutes, then transfer to a wire rack to cool completely.

5 Break up the chocolates in two separate small bowls and heat over a pan of simmering water until melted. Alternatively, melt for 2–3 minutes in the microwave.

6 When the Florentines are cold, spread the base of half of them with dark chocolate and the other half with white chocolate. Decorate, if liked, with the prongs of a fork in a rippled pattern. Leave, chocolate-sides up, to cool on the rack.

7 Store in an airtight container.

Plain Dunkers

Makes about 16

50 g/2 oz/½ cup plain (all-purpose) flour
40 g/1½ oz/⅓ cup ground rice
15 g/½ oz/2 tbsp fine oatmeal
15 g/½ oz/1 tbsp butter or margarine, plus extra for greasing
40 g/1½ oz/3 tbsp caster (superfine) sugar
2.5 ml/½ tsp vanilla essence (extract)
30–45 ml/2–3 tbsp milk

1 Mix the flour, ground rice and oatmeal together in a bowl. Rub in the butter or margarine using the fingertips.

2 Mix in the sugar and vanilla and stir in enough of the milk, a little at a time, to form a firm dough.

3 Knead gently on a lightly floured surface. Roll out to about 3 mm/⅛ in and cut into rounds using a 6 cm/2½ in cutter.

4 Lightly grease two baking (cookie) sheets. Arrange the biscuits on the sheets and prick attractively with a fork.

5 Bake one above the other in a preheated oven at 180°C/350°F/gas 4/fan oven 160°C for about 15 minutes until lightly golden, swapping the sheets over half way through cooking.

6 Remove from the oven and allow to cool slightly, then transfer to a wire rack to cool. Store in an airtight container.

Peanut and Oat Crispies

Makes 24

50 g/2 oz/¼ cup soft tub margarine
25 g/1 oz/2 tbsp caster (superfine) sugar
50 g/2 oz/¼ cup light brown sugar
60 ml/4 tbsp peanut butter
2.5 ml/½ tsp vanilla essence (extract)
1 egg, beaten
40 g/1½ oz/⅓ cup self-raising (self-rising) flour
A pinch of bicarbonate of soda (baking soda)
15 g/½ oz/2 tbsp oat bran
24 roasted peanuts, to decorate

1 Beat the margarine, sugars, peanut butter and vanilla essence together until fluffy.

2 Beat in the egg.

3 Stir in the flour, bicarbonate of soda and oat bran until thoroughly blended.

4 Line two baking (cookie) sheets with non-stick baking parchment. Put teaspoonfuls of the mixture well apart on the sheets. Bake one above the other in a preheated oven at 180°C/350°F/gas 4/fan oven 160°C for 10–12 minutes until evenly golden brown. Half way through cooking, remove the sheets from the oven and put a peanut in the centre of each biscuit. Return them to the oven, swapping over the position of the sheets, to complete the cooking time.

5 Remove from the oven and allow to cool for a few minutes before transferring to a wire rack to cool completely. Store in an airtight container.

Stem Ginger and Orange Cookies

Makes about 12

50 g/2 oz/¹/₂ cup self-raising (self-rising) flour
1.5 ml/¹/₄ tsp ground ginger
A good pinch of mixed (apple-pie) spice
25 g/1 oz/2 tbsp butter or margarine, cut into small pieces,
plus extra for greasing
20 g/³/₄ oz/1¹/₂ tbsp caster (superfine) sugar
Finely grated zest and juice of ¹/₂ small orange
10 ml/2 tsp stem ginger syrup
1 piece of stem ginger in syrup, drained and finely chopped

1   Sift the flour and spices into a bowl.

2   Add the butter or margarine and rub in using the fingertips until the mixture resembles breadcrumbs.

3   Stir in the sugar and orange zest. Stir in the ginger syrup and ginger, then add enough of the orange juice to form a stiff paste.

4   Roll out very thinly on a lightly floured surface and cut into rounds using a 5 cm/2 in cutter, re-kneading and rolling the trimmings as necessary.

5   Transfer to two lightly greased baking (cookie) sheets and bake one above the other in a preheated oven at 180°C/350°F/gas 4/fan oven 160°C for about 10–12 minutes until golden brown, swapping the sheets over half way through cooking.

6   Remove from the oven and allow to cool slightly, then transfer to a wire rack to cool completely. Store in an airtight container.

Moist and Crumbly Bites

All these biscuits have a cake-like quality that
makes them ideal to enjoy with afternoon tea or
in place of a dessert after a family meal.
But they can, of course, be enjoyed at any
time of day.

Fig and Almond Slices

Makes 10

For the base:
75 g/3 oz/³⁄₄ cup plain (all-purpose) flour
25 g/1 oz/2 tbsp caster (superfine) sugar
50 g/2 oz/¹⁄₄ cup softened butter or soft tub margarine, plus extra for greasing
75 g/3 oz/¹⁄₂ cup dried figs, chopped
For the topping:
50 g/2 oz/¹⁄₄ cup butter or margarine
50 g/2 oz/¹⁄₄ cup caster (superfine) sugar
1 egg, beaten
50 g/2 oz/¹⁄₂ cup ground almonds

1   Grease and line an 18 cm/7 in square shallow baking tin (pan) with non-stick baking parchment.

2   Make the base. Mix the flour and sugar together in a bowl. Mash in the butter or margarine with a fork and work in the figs.

3   Press this mixture into the prepared tin.

4   Make the topping. Beat the butter or margarine and sugar together until fluffy. Beat in the egg, a little at a time, beating well after each addition. Stir in the almonds. Spread over the mixture in the tin.

5   Bake in a preheated oven at 190°C/375°F/gas 5/fan oven 170°C for about 40 minutes until set and golden brown.

6   Remove from the oven and allow to cool slightly, then cut into fingers and transfer to a wire rack to cool completely. Store in an airtight container.

Chocolate Pecan Brownies

You can make plain chocolate brownies by omitting the nuts.

Makes 15

100 g/4 oz/½ cup light brown sugar

25 g/1 oz/2 tbsp butter or margarine, plus extra for greasing

30 ml/2 tbsp water

300 g/11 oz/2¾ cups plain (semi-sweet) chocolate, fairly finely chopped

5 ml/1 tsp vanilla essence (extract)

2 large eggs, beaten

65 g/2½ oz/scant ¾ cup plain (all-purpose) flour

1.5 ml/¼ tsp bicarbonate of soda (baking soda)

1.5 ml/¼ tsp salt

15 g/½ oz/2 tbsp oat bran

50 g/2 oz/½ cup pecans, chopped

1   Grease an 18 cm x 28 cm/7 in x 11 in baking tin (pan) and line with non-stick baking parchment so it stands up about 5 cm/2 in all round.

2   Put the sugar, butter or margarine and water in a saucepan and heat gently, stirring until melted. Remove from the heat and stir in half of the chocolate until melted.

3   Beat in the vanilla and eggs.

4   Sift the flour, bicarbonate of soda and salt over the surface and sprinkle on the bran. Stir in thoroughly.

5   Fold in the remaining chopped chocolate and the pecans. Turn into the prepared tin and spread evenly.

6   Bake in a preheated oven at 180°C/350°F/gas 4/fan oven 160°C for about 35 minutes until the mixture feels firm to the touch.

7   Remove from the oven and allow to cool slightly, then lift the whole slab on to a wire rack to cool completely before cutting into squares. Store in an airtight container.

Raspberry Oat Squares

Makes 15

225 g/8 oz/2 cups self-raising (self-rising) flour
2.5 ml/½ tsp salt
175 g/6 oz/¾ cup butter or margarine, cut into pieces, plus extra for greasing
175 g/6 oz/1½ cups Superfast Oats
175 g/6 oz/¾ cup caster (superfine) sugar
300 g/11 oz/1 medium can of raspberries, drained

1   Put the flour and salt in a bowl. Add the butter or margarine and rub in using the fingertips until the mixture resembles breadcrumbs. Stir in the oats and sugar.

2   Grease an 18 cm x 28 cm/7 in x 11 in shallow baking tin (pan) and press half the oat mixture into the tin.

3   Spread the raspberries over the surface, then cover with the remaining oat mixture, pressing down well.

4   Bake in a preheated oven at 200°C/400°F/gas 6/fan oven 180°C for 30 minutes until golden.

5   Remove from the oven and allow to cool for 15 minutes, then cut into squares and transfer to a wire rack to cool completely. Store in an airtight container in the fridge.

Date and Apple Squares

Makes 15

100 g/4 oz/½ cup butter or margarine, plus extra for greasing
100 g/4 oz/½ cup light brown sugar
15 ml/1 tbsp golden (light corn) syrup
100 g/4 oz/1 cup wholemeal self-raising (self-rising) flour
100 g/4 oz/1 cup Superfast Oats
2.5 ml/½ tsp bicarbonate of soda (baking soda)
2 eating (dessert) apples, peeled, cored and chopped
25 g/1 oz/3 tbsp chopped cooking dates
A little caster (superfine) sugar for dusting

1   Put the butter or margarine, sugar and syrup in a saucepan and heat gently, stirring occasionally, until melted.

2   Stir in the flour, oats and bicarbonate of soda.

3   Grease an 18 cm x 28 cm/7 in x 11 in shallow baking tin (pan) and press half the oat mixture into the tin.

4   Mix the apples and dates together and spread over the oat mixture. Scatter the remaining oat mixture over and press down lightly.

5   Bake in a preheated oven at 180°C/350°F/gas 4/fan oven 160°C for about 30 minutes until golden brown.

6   Remove from the oven and cool for a few minutes, then cut into squares. Leave to cool completely, then store in an airtight container in the fridge.

Pine Nut Cinnamon Cookies

Makes 15

50 g/2 oz/¼ cup butter or margarine, plus extra for greasing
50 g/2 oz/¼ cup caster (superfine) sugar
10 ml/2 tsp golden (light corn) syrup
1 egg, beaten
100 g/4 oz/1 cup plain (all-purpose) flour
A pinch of salt
5 ml/1 tsp baking powder
5 ml/1 tsp ground cinnamon
50 g/2 oz/½ cup fine oatmeal
25 g/1 oz/¼ cup pine nuts

1   Beat the butter or margarine and sugar together until light and fluffy.

2   Beat in the syrup and egg.

3   Sift the flour, salt, baking powder and cinnamon into the bowl and sprinkle the oatmeal over. Work in to form a soft dough. Wrap in clingfilm (plastic wrap) and chill for at least 30 minutes.

4   Grease two baking (cookie) sheets. Shape the mixture into 15 balls and place well apart on the sheets. Press the pine nuts gently on top.

5   Bake one above the other in a preheated oven at 180°C/ 350°F/gas 4/fan oven 160°C for about 15 minutes until golden brown, swapping the sheets over half way through cooking.

6   Remove from the oven and allow to cool slightly, then transfer to a wire rack to cool completely. Store in an airtight container.

Sticky Ginger Nut Brownies

Makes 15

200 g/7 oz/1¾ cups plain (all-purpose) flour
25 g/1 oz/¼ cup fine oatmeal
2.5 ml/½ tsp salt
2.5 ml/½ tsp baking powder
2.5 ml/½ tsp bicarbonate of soda (baking soda)
10 ml/2 tsp ground ginger
50 g/2 oz/½ cup chopped walnuts
175 g/6 oz/¾ cup dark brown sugar
75 g/3 oz/⅓ cup butter or margarine, plus extra for greasing
30 ml/2 tbsp black treacle (molasses)
150 ml/¼ pt/⅔ cup milk
1 egg
60 ml/4 tbsp water

1 Grease an 18 cm x 28 cm/7 in x 11 in shallow baking tin (pan) and line with non-stick baking parchment.

2 Mix the flour, oatmeal, salt, baking powder, bicarbonate of soda, ginger and nuts in a bowl.

3 Put 100 g/4 oz/½ cup of the sugar, the butter or margarine and the treacle in a saucepan and heat gently, stirring occasionally, until melted. Remove from the heat. Stir in the milk, then whisk in the egg.

4 Pour the mixture into the dry ingredients and mix well.

5 Turn into the prepared tin and level the surface. Bake in a preheated oven at 160°C/325°F/gas 3/fan oven 145°C for 30 minutes until the centre feels firm to the touch.

6 Remove from the oven and allow to cool in the tin for at least 5 minutes, then turn the slab out on to a wire rack, remove the paper and leave to cool completely.

7　Heat the remaining sugar with the water in a small saucepan gently until the sugar dissolves. Boil for 3 minutes until the syrup coats the back of a spoon. Spoon over the slab and cut into squares. Store in an airtight container.

Cherry Streusels

Makes about 16

100 g/4 oz/$\frac{1}{2}$ cup butter or margarine, plus extra for greasing
30 ml/2 tbsp golden (light corn) syrup
50 g/2 oz/$\frac{1}{4}$ cup caster (superfine) sugar
100 g/4 oz/1 cup Superfast Oats
50 g/2 oz/$\frac{1}{2}$ cup plain (all-purpose) flour
1 egg
1 eating (dessert) apple, peeled, cored and chopped
75 g/3 oz/$\frac{1}{3}$ cup glacé (candied) cherries, chopped
75 g/3 oz/$\frac{1}{2}$ cup sultanas (golden raisins)
Halved glacé cherries, to decorate

1　Melt the butter or margarine, syrup and sugar in a saucepan. Remove from the heat.

2　Stir in the oats and flour, then mix in the egg, apple, cherries and sultanas.

3　Grease two baking (cookie) sheets. Drop heaped dessert-spoonfuls of the mixture on the sheets and top each with half a glacé cherry.

4　Bake one above the other in a preheated oven at 180°C/ 350°F/ gas 4/fan oven 160°C for 10–12 minutes until golden, swapping the sheets over half way through cooking.

5　Remove from the oven and allow to cool slightly, then transfer to a wire rack to cool completely. Store in an airtight container in the fridge.

Coffee and Walnut Meringue Tops

Makes 12

For the base

50 g/2 oz/¼ cup light brown sugar

100 g/4 oz/½ cup butter or margarine

10 ml/2 tsp instant coffee granules

15 ml/1 tbsp water

1 egg

175 g/6 oz/1½ cups plain (all-purpose) flour

15 g/½ oz/2 tbsp wheat or oat bran

2.5 ml/½ tsp salt

For the meringue tops:

1 egg white

5 ml/1 tsp instant coffee granules

5 ml/1 tsp water

15 ml/1 tbsp golden (light corn) syrup

100 g/4 oz/½ cup caster (superfine) sugar

50 g/2 oz/½ cup walnut pieces, chopped

1 Make the base. Put the sugar and butter or margarine in a saucepan and heat gently, stirring occasionally, until melted. Leave to cool.

2 Line an 18 cm/7 in square shallow baking tin (pan) with non-stick baking parchment.

3 Dissolve the coffee in the water and beat in the egg. Beat into the cooled sugar mixture.

4 Sprinkle the flour, bran and salt over the surface and mix in. Spread in the prepared tin (pan).

5 Bake in a preheated oven at 190°C/375°F/gas 5/fan oven 170°C for 10 minutes.

6   Meanwhile, make the meringue tops. Whisk the egg white until stiff. Dissolve the coffee in the water and whisk into the egg white with the syrup.

7   Whisk in the caster sugar until stiff and glossy, then fold in the nuts.

8   Spread this mixture over the baked mixture in the tin and bake for 20 minutes until golden and set.

9   Remove from the oven and allow to cool for 15 minutes, then cut into pieces and leave to cool completely in the tin. Store in an airtight container.

Iced and Sandwich Biscuits

This is where you'll find classics such as Custard Creams and sensational speciality biscuits like Chocolate Kisses – meltingly crisp buttons, sandwiched with chocolate nut spread. Heavenly!

Orange Oat Trickles

Makes about 20

100 g/4 oz/½ cup butter or margarine, softened,
plus extra for greasing
75 g/3 oz/⅓ cup caster (superfine) sugar
30 ml/2 tbsp golden (light corn) syrup
Finely grated zest and juice of 1 small orange
100 g/4 oz/1 cup Superfast Oats
100 g/4 oz/1 cup self-raising (self-rising) flour
2.5 ml/½ tsp bicarbonate of soda (baking soda)
100 g/4 oz/⅔ cup icing (confectioners') sugar
A few drops of orange food colouring (optional)

1 Put the butter or margarine, sugar, syrup and orange zest in a bowl and beat until fluffy.

2 Work in the oats, flour and bicarbonate of soda.

3 Grease two baking (cookie) sheets. Shape the mixture into small balls and place well apart on the sheets. Flatten slightly.

4 Bake one above the other in a preheated oven at 180°C/ 350°F/gas 4/fan oven 160°C for about 15 minutes until golden, swapping the sheets over half way through cooking.

5 Remove from the oven and allow to cool slightly, then transfer to a wire rack to cool completely.

6 Sift the icing sugar into a bowl. Add 15 ml/1 tbsp of the orange juice and mix until thick and creamy, adding a few drops of food colouring, if liked.

7 Trickle over the cold biscuits in a zig-zag pattern and leave to set. Store in an airtight container.

Vanilla Jces

Makes about 10

For the biscuits:

100 g/4 oz/½ cup butter, softened, plus extra for greasing

50 g/2 oz/¼ cup caster (superfine) sugar,
plus extra for sprinkling

2.5 ml/½ tsp vanilla essence (extract)

175 g/6 oz/1½ cups plain (all-purpose) flour, plus extra for dusting

For the icing (frosting):

50 g/2 oz/¼ cup butter, softened

100 g/4 oz/⅔ cup icing (confectioners') sugar

A few drops of vanilla essence

1   Make the biscuits. Beat the butter, sugar and vanilla together until light and fluffy.

2   Sift the flour over the surface and fold in with a metal spoon. Draw the mixture together into a ball and knead on a lightly floured surface until smooth.

3   Cut the dough in half and roll out one half to about 5 mm/ ¼ in thick. Cut out 10 rounds using a 5 cm/2 in cutter, re-kneading and rolling the trimmings as necessary. Repeat with the other half of the dough.

4   Place the biscuits on a lightly greased baking (cookie) sheet. Prick attractively with a fork to decorate.

5   Bake in a preheated oven at 160°C/325°F/gas 3/fan oven 145°C for 15 minutes until a pale biscuit colour.

6   Remove from the oven and allow to cool for 10 minutes, then transfer to a wire rack to cool completely.

7   Make the icing. Beat the butter until soft. Sift some of the icing sugar over and beat until blended. Repeat until all the icing sugar is used. Beat in vanilla essence to taste.

8   Sandwich the cold biscuits together in pairs with the icing. Store in an airtight container.

Coffee Treats

Makes about 16

For the biscuits:
75 g/3 oz/⅓ cup butter or margarine, plus extra for greasing
50 g/2 oz/¼ cup caster (superfine) sugar
175 g/6 oz/1½ cups plain (all-purpose) flour
A pinch of salt
For the icing (frosting):
10 ml/2 tsp instant coffee granules
15 ml/1 tbsp water
100 g 4 oz/⅔ cup icing (confectioners') sugar, sifted

1 Make the biscuits. Beat the butter and sugar together until light and fluffy.

2 Work in the flour and salt.

3 Knead gently on a lightly floured surface and roll out thinly. Cut into rectangles about 5 cm x 7.5 cm/2 in x 3 in. Transfer to two greased baking (cookie) sheets. Re-knead and cut any trimmings as necessary.

4 Bake one above the other in a preheated oven at 150°C/ 300°F/gas 2/fan oven 135°C for about 25 minutes, swapping the sheets over half way through cooking, until lightly golden round the edges.

5 Remove from the oven and allow to cool for 5 minutes, then transfer to a wire rack to cool completely.

6 Make the icing. Blend the coffee with 10 ml/2 tsp of the water and mix in the icing sugar, adding enough extra water to form a thick, creamy consistency.

7 Spread a little in an oval shape on the top of each biscuit and leave to set. Store in an airtight container.

Galas

Makes 24

100 g/4 oz/½ cup butter or margarine, plus extra for greasing
100 g/4 oz/½ cup caster (superfine) sugar,
plus extra for sprinkling
1 egg, beaten
225 g/8 oz/2 cups plain (all-purpose) flour
100 g/4 oz/1 cup fine oatmeal
A few drops of vanilla essence (extract)
85 g/3½ oz/1 large Mars bar
30 ml/2 tbsp milk

1   Beat the butter and sugar together until light and fluffy.

2   Beat in the egg, a little at a time, beating well after each addition.

3   Add the flour, oatmeal and the vanilla essence and work in to form a firm dough.

4   Knead gently on a lightly floured surface, roll out and cut into 48 rounds using a 5 cm/2 in cutter, re-kneading and rolling the trimmings as necessary. Transfer to two greased baking (cookie) sheets.

5   Bake one above the other in a preheated oven at 180°C/350°F/gas 4/fan oven 160°C for about 15 minutes until golden brown, swapping the sheets over half way through cooking.

6   Remove from the oven and allow to cool slightly, then transfer to a wire rack to cool completely.

7   Break up the Mars bar and put in a saucepan with the milk. Heat very gently, stirring, until melted.

8   Sandwich the biscuits together in pairs with the Mars bar mixture and sprinkle the top with a little caster sugar. Store in an airtight container.

Lime or Lemon Tops

Makes 24

For the biscuits:
100 g/4 oz/1 cup cornflour (cornstarch)
100 g/4 oz/1 cup plain (all-purpose) flour
175 g/6 oz/¾ cup butter or margarine, cut into small pieces
75 g/3 oz/⅓ cup caster (superfine) sugar
Finely grated zest of 1 lime or ½ small lemon
For the icing (frosting):
75 g/3 oz/⅓ cup butter or margarine
225 g/8 oz/1⅓ cups icing (confectioners') sugar, sifted
Juice of 1 lime or ½ small lemon
Crystallised lime or lemon slices, to decorate

1　Make the biscuits. Sift the flours in a bowl. Add the butter or margarine and rub in using the fingertips.

2　Stir in the sugar and the lime or lemon zest and knead together to form a ball.

3　Roll out on a lightly floured surface and cut into rounds using a 6 cm/2½ in cutter, re-kneading and rolling the trimmings as necessary. Transfer to two greased baking (cookie) sheets.

4　Bake one above the other in a preheated oven at 180°C/ 350°F/gas 4/fan oven 160°C for 15 minutes until golden brown, swapping the sheets over half way through cooking.

5　Remove from the oven and allow to cool slightly, then transfer to a wire rack to cool completely.

6　Make the icing. Mash the butter or margarine until soft, then work in the icing sugar and juice to form a soft icing.

7　Pipe or spread on the biscuits and top each with a small piece of crystallised lime or lemon slice to decorate. Store in an airtight container.

Apricot Almond Jammies

Makes about 16

75 g/3 oz/⅓ cup softened butter or soft tub margarine,
plus extra for greasing
50 g/2 oz/¼ cup caster (superfine) sugar
2.5 ml/½ tsp almond or vanilla essence (extract)
75 g/3 oz/¾ cup ground almonds
75 g/3 oz/¾ cup plain (all-purpose) flour
A little beaten egg white, to glaze
15 g/½ oz/2 tbsp chopped almonds
45–60 ml/3–4 tbsp apricot jam (conserve)

1   Cream the butter or margarine and sugar together with the almond or vanilla essence until light and fluffy.

2   Work in the ground almonds and flour until the mixture forms a ball. Wrap in clingfilm (plastic wrap) and chill for at least 30 minutes.

3   Cut the dough in half. Roll out one half on a lightly floured surface to about 5 mm/¼ in thickness. Cut into rounds using a 6 cm/2½ in fluted cutter.

4   Roll out the remaining dough and repeat the process. Cut a 2 cm/¾ in round out of the centre of half the rounds using a bottle top or the wide end of a piping tube (tip) as a guide. Re-knead the trimmings to make more circles and cut out the centres of half of them as before.

5   Carefully transfer the rounds and rings to greased baking (cookie) sheets lined with non-stick baking parchment. Brush the tops of the rings only with beaten egg white and sprinkle them with the chopped almonds.

6   Bake one above the other in a preheated oven at 180°C/ 350°F/gas 4/fan oven 160°C for 12–15 minutes, swapping the sheets over half way through cooking.

7   Remove from the oven and allow to cool slightly, then transfer to a wire rack to cool completely. When cold, spread the rounds with apricot jam and sandwich together with the rings. Store in an airtight container.

Jammy Sangers

Makes 14

100 g/4 oz/1 cup cornflour (cornstarch)
100 g/4 oz/1 cup plain (all-purpose) flour
200 g/7 oz/generous 1 cup icing (confectioners') sugar
225 g/8 oz/1 cup softened butter or soft tub margarine
45 ml/3 tbsp seedless raspberry jam (clear conserve)
2.5 ml/½ tsp vanilla essence (extract)

1   Sift the flours and 75 g/3 oz/½ cup of the icing sugar together in a bowl. Add 175 g/6 oz/¾ cup of the butter or margarine and work in with a fork to form a dough. Wrap in foil or clingfilm (plastic wrap) and chill for 30 minutes.

2   Roll out the dough fairly thinly and cut into 28 rounds using a 6 cm/2½ in cutter, re-kneading and rolling the trimmings as necessary. Place a little apart on two baking (cookie) sheets lined with non-stick baking parchment.

3   Make a hole in the centre of half the rounds with the end of a wooden spoon. Spoon a little jam into each hole.

4   Bake one above the other in a preheated oven at 160°C/ 325°F/gas 3/fan oven 145°C for 20–25 minutes until lightly golden, swapping the sheets over half way through cooking.

5   Remove from the oven and leave to cool on the baking sheets.

6   Meanwhile, sift the remaining icing sugar and work in the remaining butter or margarine and the vanilla essence.

7   Spread this mixture on the underside of the plain biscuits. Carefully lift the jam-filled biscuits off the paper and place on top. Store in an airtight container.

Iced Garibaldi Biscuits

If you prefer a sweeter icing, use water instead of lemon juice.

Makes 12–16

For the biscuits:

175 g/6 oz/1½ cups self-raising (self-rising) flour

A good pinch of salt

40 g/1½ oz/3 tbsp butter or margarine, cut into small pieces,
plus extra for greasing

40 g/1½ oz/3 tbsp caster (superfine) sugar, plus extra for
sprinkling

45 ml/3 tbsp milk, plus extra for brushing

50 g/2 oz/⅓ cup currants

For the icing (frosting):

100 g/4 oz/⅔ cup icing (confectioners') sugar, sifted

15 ml/1 tbsp lemon juice

1 Make the biscuits. Sift the flour and salt into a bowl.

2 Add the butter or margarine and rub in using the fingertips.

3 Stir in the sugar, then mix with enough of the milk to form a firm dough. Knead gently on a lightly floured surface.

4 Roll out thinly to a rectangle about 3 mm/⅛ in thick. Cut the rectangle in half widthways and scatter the currants over half the dough. Brush the other half with water, then carefully invert it on top of the currants and roll lightly with the rolling pin to seal the two halves together.

5 Cut into triangles or rectangles and transfer to a greased baking (cookie) sheet. Brush with milk and sprinkle with caster sugar.

6 Bake in a preheated oven at 190°C/375°F/gas 5/fan oven 170°C for 12–15 minutes until golden brown. Remove from the oven and transfer to a wire rack to cool.

7 Make the icing. Mix the icing sugar with enough lemon juice to form a thick creamy consistency. Spread a little on each biscuit and leave to set. Store in an airtight container.

Chocolate Kisses

For a change from sandwich biscuits, spread the undersides of each one with melted chocolate instead (you'll need about 100 g/4 oz/1 cup).

Makes 8

75 g/3 oz/³⁄₄ cup plain (all-purpose) flour
50 g/2 oz/¹⁄₄ cup butter or margarine, cut into small pieces, plus extra for greasing
50 g/2 oz/¹⁄₄ cup caster (superfine) sugar
About 15 ml/1 tbsp chocolate hazelnut (filbert) spread

1 Put the flour in a bowl. Add the butter or margarine and rub in with the fingertips.

2 Stir in the sugar, then draw together with the hands to form a ball.

3 Knead gently, then shape into 16 small balls.

4 Grease a baking (cookie) sheet. Place the balls a little apart on the sheet and flatten with a fork.

5 Bake in a preheated oven at 190°C/375°F/gas 5/fan oven 170°C for about 6–7 minutes until golden brown.

6 Remove from the oven and transfer to a wire rack to cool.

7 When cold, sandwich the biscuits together in pairs with the chocolate spread. Store in an airtight container.

Honey Pistachio Chocolate Dips

You can use ground almonds or hazelnuts (filberts), if you prefer.

Makes 12

75 g/3 oz/³/₄ cup shelled pistachios
100 g/4 oz/¹/₂ cup butter, softened, plus extra for greasing
50 g/2 oz/¹/₄ cup caster (superfine) sugar
150 g/5 oz/1¹/₄ cups plain (all-purpose) flour
100 g/4 oz/1 cup milk chocolate
60 ml/4 tbsp thick honey

1 Grind the pistachios in a blender or food processor.

2 Beat the butter and sugar together in a bowl until light and fluffy.

3 Add about a third of the nuts, then a third of the flour and fold in. Repeat with the remaining nuts and flour to form a soft but not sticky dough. Cover the bowl with clingfilm (plastic wrap) and chill for at least 30 minutes.

4 Roll out the dough thinly on a lightly floured surface and cut into 24 rounds using a 6 cm/2¹/₂ in cutter, re-kneading and rolling the trimmings as necessary.

5 Place on two greased baking (cookie) sheets and bake one above the other in a preheated oven at 180°C/350°F/gas 4/fan oven 160°C for 20–30 minutes, swapping the sheets over after 15 minutes.

6 Remove from the oven and allow to cool slightly, then transfer to a wire rack to cool completely.

7 Break up the chocolate and melt in a bowl over a pan of simmering water. Alternatively, melt the chocolate briefly in the microwave.

8 Sandwich the biscuits together in pairs with the honey, then dip half of each sandwich in the melted chocolate. Leave to dry on non-stick baking parchment. Store in an airtight container.

Bourbon Creams

Makes 12–16

For the biscuits:

75 g/3 oz/⅓ cup butter or margarine, plus extra for greasing

75 g/3 oz/⅓ cup caster (superfine) sugar

1 egg

1.5 ml/¼ tsp vanilla essence (extract)

225 g/8 oz/2 cups plain (all-purpose) flour

25 g/1 oz/¼ cup cocoa (unsweetened chocolate) powder

1.5 ml/¼ tsp salt

For the filling:

50 g/2 oz/½ cup plain (semi-sweet) chocolate

25 g/1 oz/2 tbsp butter or margarine

50 g/2 oz/⅓ cup icing (confectioners') sugar, sifted

1   Make the biscuits. Beat the butter or margarine and sugar together until light and fluffy. Beat in the egg and vanilla essence.

2   Sift the flour, cocoa and salt over the surface. Mix to form a soft but not sticky dough.

3   Knead gently on a lightly floured surface. Roll out to 5 mm/¼ in thick. Cut into rectangles about 1.5 cm x 5 cm/⅔ in x 2 in.

4   Grease two baking (cookie) sheets. Transfer the biscuits to the sheets and prick with a fork. Bake one above the other in a preheated oven at 190°C/375°F/gas 5/fan oven 170°C for about 10–15 minutes until firm, swapping the sheets over half way through cooking.

5   Remove from the oven and allow to cool slightly, then transfer to a wire rack to cool completely.

6   Make the filling. Break up the chocolate and melt it in a bowl over a pan of hot water, or in the microwave.

7   Beat the butter or margarine in a bowl until soft. Beat in the icing sugar and melted chocolate. Use to sandwich the biscuits together in pairs. Store in an airtight container.

Custard Creams

Makes 12

For the biscuits:
175 g/6 oz/³/₄ cup softened butter or soft tub margarine,
plus extra for greasing
50 g/2 oz/¹/₃ cup icing (confectioners') sugar
50 g/2 oz/¹/₂ cup custard powder
225 g/8 oz/2 cups plain (all-purpose) flour
5 ml/1 tsp baking powder
A good pinch of salt
For the filling:
50 g/2 oz/¹/₄ cup butter or margarine
100 g/4 oz/²/₃ cup icing sugar
15 g/¹/₂ oz/2 tbsp custard powder
2.5 ml/¹/₂ tsp vanilla essence (extract)

1 Make the biscuits. Beat the butter or margarine with the icing sugar and custard powder until soft and fluffy. Sift the flour, baking powder and salt over the surface and work in to form a soft dough. Wrap in clingfilm (plastic wrap) and chill for at least 30 minutes.

2 Knead gently on a lightly floured surface. Roll out to about 5 mm/¹/₄ in thick and cut into 5 cm/2 in squares.

3 Grease two baking (cookie) sheets. Transfer the biscuits to the sheets and prick with a fork. Bake one above the other in a preheated oven at 160°C/325°F/gas 3/fan oven 145°C for about 20 minutes or until a pale biscuit colour, swapping the sheets over half way through cooking.

4 Remove from the oven and allow to cool slightly, then transfer to a wire rack to cool completely.

5 Make the filling. Beat the butter or margarine until soft. Sift the icing sugar and custard powder over. Work into the butter until smooth. Beat in the vanilla. Sandwich the biscuits together with the filling. Store in an airtight container.

Melt-in-the-Mouth Biscuits

From buttery Viennese Fingers to nutty, fluffy Almond Macaroons, all these biscuits have a crisp bite but a melting quality that make them irresistible!

Petticoat Oat Tails

Makes 8

75 g/3 oz/¹/₃ cup butter
50 g/2 oz/¹/₄ cup caster (superfine) sugar
50 g/2 oz/¹/₂ cup plain (all-purpose) flour
25 g/1 oz/¹/₄ cup fine oatmeal
25 g/1 oz/¹/₄ cup ground rice or rice flour

1 Beat the butter with half the sugar. Work in the flour, oatmeal and rice. Reserve 15 ml/1 tbsp of the remaining sugar for sprinkling, then work the remainder into the dough.

2 Press into a fluted flan ring set on a baking (cookie) sheet, or press into a round on the sheet and crimp the edge all round between the finger and thumb. Prick with a fork.

3 Bake in a preheated oven at 150°C/300°F/gas 2/fan oven 135°C for about 40 minutes until a very pale biscuit colour.

4 Remove from the oven and mark into eight wedges. Dust with the remaining sugar and leave to cool completely before cutting into pieces. Store in an airtight container.

Hazelnut Chocolate Chip Shortbread

For extra-rich shortbread, instead of dusting it with sugar, spread it with chocolate hazelnut spread once cold before separating it into wedges.

Makes 8

175 g/6 oz/1½ cups plain (all-purpose) flour

100 g/4 oz/½ cup butter, cut into small pieces

50 g/2 oz/¼ cup caster (superfine) sugar, plus extra for dusting

25 g/1 oz/¼ cup chocolate chips (or slab chocolate, chopped)

15 g/½ oz/2 tbsp chopped hazelnuts (filberts)

1   Put the flour in a bowl. Add the butter and rub in using the fingertips until the mixture resembles breadcrumbs. Stir in the sugar.

2   Add the chocolate and nuts and knead the mixture until it forms a ball.

3   Press the dough into a 20 cm/8 in flan ring set on a baking (cookie) sheet. Prick attractively with a fork.

4   Bake in a preheated oven at 160°C/325°F/gas 3/fan oven 145°C for about 25 minutes until pale biscuit coloured.

5   Remove from the oven and allow to cool slightly, then mark into eight wedges. Dust with caster sugar. Leave to cool completely before cutting into wedges. Store in an airtight container.

Cream Buttons

These are also delicious sandwiched in pairs with whipped cream and crushed strawberries or a chocolate butter cream.

Makes about 28

50 g/2 oz/¼ cup butter
15 ml/1 tbsp double (heavy) cream
50 g/2 oz/½ cup plain (all-purpose) flour
60 ml/4 tbsp caster (superfine) sugar

1 Beat the butter until soft.

2 Beat in the cream, then stir in the flour. Cover the bowl with clingfilm (plastic wrap) and chill for at least 1 hour.

3 Roll out the dough very thinly (about 3 mm/⅛ in) on a lightly floured surface. Dredge all over with half the caster sugar. Cut into rounds using a 4 cm/1½ in cutter.

4 Invert on a baking (cookie) sheet lined with non-stick baking parchment and dredge with the remaining sugar. Prick with a fork.

5 Bake in a preheated oven at 190°C/375°F/gas 5/fan oven 170°C for about 10 minutes until they are golden and slightly puffed up.

6 Remove from the oven and allow to cool slightly, then transfer to a wire rack to cool completely. Store in an airtight container.

Viennese Whirls

Makes 16

150 g/5 oz/²⁄₃ cup softened butter or soft tub margarine,
plus extra for greasing
40 g/1½ oz/¼ cup icing (confectioners') sugar
100 g/4 oz/1 cup plain (all-purpose) flour
50 g/2 oz/½ cup cornflour (cornstarch)
2.5 ml/½ tsp vanilla essence (extract)
4 glacé (candied) cherries, quartered, to decorate

1 Beat the butter or margarine with the icing sugar until light and fluffy.

2 Beat in the flours and vanilla essence.

3 Spoon the mixture into a piping (pastry) bag fitted with a star tube (tip). Pipe whirls a little apart on two lightly greased baking (cookie) sheets. Top each with a quartered glacé cherry.

4 Bake one above the other in a preheated oven at 190°C/375°F/gas 5/fan oven 170°C for about 12 minutes or until pale golden brown, swapping the sheets over half way through cooking.

5 Remove from the oven and allow to cool slightly, then transfer to a wire rack to cool completely. Store in an airtight container.

Viennese Fingers

These can also be sandwiched together in pairs with a little buttercream, if liked

Makes about 20

100 g/4 oz/½ cup butter, plus extra for greasing
25 g/1 oz/3 tbsp icing (confectioners') sugar
150 g/5 oz/1¼ cups plain (all-purpose) flour
100 g/4 oz/1 cup plain (semi-sweet) chocolate

1 Grease two baking (cookie) sheets.

2 Beat the butter and icing sugar together until fluffy. Work in the flour to form a paste.

3 Put the mixture in a piping (pastry) bag with a large star tube (tip) and pipe strips about 7.5 cm/3 in long a little apart on the prepared sheets.

4 Bake one above the other in a preheated oven at 190°C/ 375°F/gas 5/fan oven 170°C for 10–15 minutes until pale golden brown, swapping the sheets over half way through cooking.

5 Remove from the oven and transfer to a wire rack to cool.

6 Break the chocolate up and place in a bowl. Stand it over a pan of hot water to melt. Alternatively, melt the chocolate briefly in the microwave.

7 Dip one end of the biscuits in the melted chocolate. When hardened, dip the other end in the chocolate (if you do both ends at once, you'll get in a gooey mess!). Leave until firm. Store in an airtight container.

Spiced Toasted Oat and Cherry Meringues

It was tricky to decide which category these fall into. The crisp meringue does melt in the mouth, but then you have the delicious nutty-tasting oats and the cherries to chew!

Makes 12

50 g/2 oz/½ cup Superfast Oats
2 egg whites
A good pinch of salt
5 ml/1 tsp cornflour (cornstarch)
2.5 ml/½ tsp mixed (apple-pie) spice
175 g/6 oz/¾ cup caster (superfine) sugar
75 g/3 oz/¾ cup multicoloured glacé (candied) cherries

1 Heat a heavy-based frying pan (skillet). Add the oats, spread out and cook until golden, stirring and turning as necessary. Tip out of the pan on to a plate to prevent further cooking.

2 Whisk the egg whites with the salt until fairly stiff. Sprinkle the cornflour and spice over and whisk again until stiff.

3 Add half the sugar and whisk until stiff and glossy. Sprinkle the remaining sugar over the surface and fold in with a metal spoon. Halve six of the cherries and reserve for decoration and chop the remainder. Reserve 15 ml/1 tbsp of the oats for decoration and sprinkle the remaining oats over the surface of the egg mixture. Add the chopped cherries and fold in with the metal spoon.

4 Line a baking (cookie) sheet with non-stick baking parchment. Put spoonfuls of the meringue a little apart on the sheet. Sprinkle with the remaining oats and top each with a halved glacé cherry.

5   Bake in a preheated oven at 120°C/250°F/gas ½/fan oven 110°C for 2 hours until crisp but still very pale. Turn off the oven and leave to cool in there.

6   Store in an airtight container.

Almond Macaroons

You can make hazelnut (filbert) macaroons in the same way, using ground hazelnuts and vanilla essence instead of almond.

Makes 10

1 egg white
75 g/3 oz/¾ cup ground almonds
75 g/3 oz/⅓ cup caster (superfine) sugar
15 ml/1 tbsp ground rice
1.5 ml/¼ tsp almond essence (extract)
10 whole blanched almonds

1   Line a baking (cookie) sheet with rice paper.

2   Whisk the egg white until very frothy but not stiff.

3   Beat in the ground almonds, sugar, ground rice and almond essence.

4   Spoon 10 mounds of the mixture well apart on the rice paper and top each with a whole almond.

5   Bake in a preheated oven at 160°C/325°F/gas 3/fan oven 145°C for about 25 minutes until pale golden brown and crisp.

6   Remove from the oven and allow to cool, then carefully cut round each macaroon with scissors. Store in an airtight container.

Lemon Thins

If you pipe these they have an attractive swirled top – but it's not essential.

Makes about 16

100 g/4 oz/½ cup butter, plus extra for greasing
50 g/2 oz/⅓ cup icing (confectioners') sugar, sifted
Finely grated zest of 1 lemon
100 g/4 oz/1 cup plain (all-purpose) flour

1   Beat the butter and icing sugar together until light and fluffy.

2   Work in the lemon zest and flour to form a paste.

3   Put the mixture in a piping (pastry) bag fitted with a large star tube (tip) and pipe swirls, well apart, on two greased baking (cookie) sheets. Alternatively, shape into small balls.

4   Bake one above the other in a preheated oven at 160°C/325°F/gas 3/fan oven 145°C for about 25 minutes until golden, swapping the sheets over half way through cooking.

5   Remove from the oven and allow to cool slightly, then transfer to a wire rack to cool completely. Store in an airtight container.

Butter Shorties

Makes about 20

65 g/2½ oz/scant ⅓ cup butter, softened, plus extra for greasing
50 g/2 oz/¼ cup caster (superfine) sugar
5 ml/1 tsp vanilla essence (extract)
100 g/4 oz/1 cup self-raising (self-rising) flour
Glacé (candied) cherries, halved, to decorate

1   Put the butter, sugar and vanilla in a bowl and beat well until light and fluffy.

2   Gradually mix in the flour to form a soft dough.

3   Grease two baking (cookie) sheets. Shape the mixture into walnut-sized balls and place a little apart on the sheets. Flatten each with a fork dipped in cold water and place half a cherry in the centre of each.

4   Bake one above the other in a preheated oven at 190°C/ 375°F/gas 5/fan oven 170°C for about 15 minutes until golden, swapping the sheets over half way through cooking.

5   Remove from the oven and transfer to a wire rack to cool. Store in an airtight container.

Chocolate Jumbles

Makes 12

100 g/4 oz/½ cup butter, plus extra for greasing

40 g/1½ oz/¼ cup icing (confectioners') sugar, sifted, plus extra for dusting

100 g/4 oz/1 cup plain (all-purpose) flour

15 g/½ oz/2 tbsp cocoa (unsweetened chocolate) powder

1   Beat the butter and icing sugar together until fluffy.

2   Sift the flour and cocoa over and work in to form a stiff paste. Put in a piping (pastry) bag fitted with a large star tube (tip). Pipe curved shapes on to two greased baking (cookie) sheets.

3   Bake in a preheated oven at 190°C/375°F/gas 5/fan oven 170°C for 10–15 minutes until firm.

4   Remove from the oven and allow to cool slightly, then transfer to a wire rack to cool completely. Dust with a little sifted icing sugar. Store in an airtight container.

Palmiers

Makes 24

75 g/3 oz/¹/₃ cup caster (superfine) sugar
225 g/8 oz puff pastry (paste), thawed if frozen
25 g/1 oz/2 tbsp butter, melted

1   Sprinkle the work surface with a little of the sugar.

2   Roll out the pastry thinly to about 25 cm x 30 cm/10 in x 12 in.

3   Brush with a little melted butter, then sprinkle liberally with some of the sugar.

4   Fold the long sides in so they nearly meet in the middle then flip one folded side over the other. Wrap in clingfilm (plastic wrap) and chill for at least 30 minutes.

5   Rinse two baking (cookie) sheets with cold water. Using a sharp knife, cut the pastry into 24 slices and place on the wetted sheets. Sprinkle with a little more of the sugar.

6   Bake one above the other in a preheated oven at 220°C/425°F/gas 7/fan oven 200°C for 10 minutes. Turn each palmier over, swap the sheets over and bake for a further 3–4 minutes until crisp and golden brown.

7   Remove from the oven and sprinkle the biscuits immediately with more sugar. Transfer them to a wire rack to cool completely. Store in an airtight container.

Blueberry Melts

Makes about 12

100 g/4 oz/½ cup butter, softened, plus extra for greasing
40 g/1½ oz/3 tbsp caster (superfine) sugar,
plus extra for sprinkling
150 g/5 oz/1¼ cups plain (all-purpose) flour
40 g/1½ oz/⅓ cup ground rice
5 ml/1 tsp finely grated lemon zest
50 g/2 oz/⅓ cup dried blueberries

1 Beat the butter and sugar until light and fluffy.

2 Work in the flour, ground rice, lemon zest and blueberries, then draw the mixture together to form a dough.

3 Using your hands, roll the dough into a sausage shape about 5 cm/2 in in diameter. Wrap in clingfilm (plastic wrap) and chill for at least 30 minutes.

4 Unwrap and cut into slices about 1 cm/½ in thick. Place the rounds well apart on a lightly greased baking (cookie) sheet.

5 Bake in a preheated oven at 160°C/325°F/gas 3/fan oven 145°C for about 40 minutes until lightly golden.

6 Remove from the oven and sprinkle with a little caster sugar. Allow to cool slightly, then transfer to a wire rack to cool completely. Store in an airtight container.

Soft and Chewy Biscuits

Some of these are chewy, soft and moist all through; others have a crisp first bite then a delicious softer texture as you munch.

Toffee Squares

Makes 24

50 g/2 oz/¼ cup butter or margarine
100 g/4 oz/1 small packet of marshmallows
30 ml/2 tbsp golden (light corn) syrup
5 ml/1 tsp lemon juice
150 g/5 oz/2½ cups crisped rice cereal
Oil for greasing

1 Put the butter or margarine, marshmallows and syrup in a heavy-based saucepan and heat gently, stirring, until melted.

2 Stir in the lemon juice and cereal.

3 Press into an oiled 18 x 28 cm/7 x 11 in Swiss roll tin (jelly roll pan), using the back of a wet spoon to level the surface.

4 Leave until cold and set firm, then cut into squares. Store in an airtight container.

Chocolate Caramel Squares

Makes 15

200 g/7 oz/1 packet of shortcake biscuits
175 g/6 oz/³/₄ cup butter, plus extra for greasing
400 g/14 oz/1 large can of sweetened condensed milk
30 ml/2 tbsp golden (light corn) syrup
200 g/7 oz/1³/₄ cups plain (semi-sweet) chocolate

1 Put the biscuits in a bag and finely crush with a rolling pin.

2 Melt 50 g/2 oz/¹/₄ cup of the butter in a saucepan. Add the biscuits and mix well.

3 Lightly grease an 18 cm x 28 cm/7 in x 11 in shallow baking tin (pan) and press the biscuits into the tin.

4 Rinse out the pan. Put the remaining butter in the pan with the condensed milk and syrup. Bring to the boil and boil, stirring constantly, for about 5 minutes until golden and the butter has blended in completely. Spoon this mixture over the biscuits and spread out.

5 Break up the chocolate and place it in a bowl over a pan of simmering water. Heat until melted, stirring occasionally. Alternatively, melt the chocolate briefly in the microwave.

6 Spread the chocolate over the caramel mixture and leave to cool, then chill until firm. Cut into squares. Store in an airtight container.

Cherry and Sultana Slices

Makes 15

150 g/5 oz/²/₃ cup butter or margarine, plus extra for greasing
175 g/6 oz/³/₄ cup dark brown sugar
15 ml/1 tbsp golden (light corn) syrup
225 g/8 oz/2 cups Superfast Oats
2.5 ml/½ tsp ground cinnamon
75 g/3 oz/½ cup sultanas (golden raisins)
75 g/3 oz/¹/₃ cup glacé (candied) cherries, quartered

1　Put the butter or margarine, sugar and syrup in a saucepan and heat, stirring occasionally, until melted.

2　Stir in the oats, cinnamon, sultanas and cherries.

3　Grease an 18 cm x 28 cm/7 in x 11 in shallow baking tin (pan). Press the mixture into the tin.

4　Bake in a preheated oven at 190°C/375°F/gas 5/fan oven 170°C for about 25 minutes until golden brown.

5　Remove from the oven and allow to cool for 10 minutes, then cut into bars and leave to cool completely before removing from the tin. Store in an airtight container.

Fruity Flapjacks

Makes 8

50 g/2 oz/¹/₄ cup butter or margarine, plus extra for greasing
60 ml/4 tbsp clear honey
175 g/6 oz/1½ cups Superfast Oats
50 g/2 oz/½ cup dried mixed fruit (fruit cake mix)

1   Melt the butter or margarine and honey in a saucepan. Stir in the oats and fruit.

2   Turn into a greased 18 cm/7 in square shallow baking tin (pan).

3   Bake in a preheated oven at 180°C/350°F/gas 4/fan oven 160°C for about 20–25 minutes until turning golden brown.

4   Remove from the oven and allow to cool for 5 minutes, then cut into fingers and leave to cool completely before removing from the tin. Store in an airtight container.

Moreish Mallow Bars

Makes 8

75 g/3 oz/⅓ cup butter or margarine, plus extra for greasing
175 g/6 oz Nice biscuits
100 g/4 oz/1 small packet of marshmallows
75 g/3 oz/⅓ cup caster (superfine) sugar
2.5 ml/½ tsp vanilla essence (extract)
1 egg

1   Grease an 18 cm/7 in square shallow baking tin (pan).

2   Melt the butter or margarine in a bowl over a pan of gently simmering water.

3   Meanwhile, crush the biscuits finely in a bag with a rolling pin. Snip the marshmallows into small pieces with wet scissors.

4   When the butter is melted, whisk in the sugar, vanilla and egg. Continue to whisk for about 20 minutes until the mixture thickens slightly. Don't allow the mixture to boil or it will curdle.

5   Stir the biscuits and marshmallows into the egg mixture, then press into the prepared tin. Leave to cool, then chill to set. Cut into eight bars. Store in an airtight container in the fridge.

Orange Drops

These are best eaten fresh as they tend to harden if stored for more than a few days.

Makes about 12

2 egg whites
100 g/4 oz/½ cup caster (superfine) sugar
100 g/4 oz/1 cup plain (all-purpose) flour
50 g/2 oz/¼ cup butter, melted
Finely grated zest of 1 orange

1 Line two baking (cookie) sheets with non-stick baking parchment.

2 Whisk the egg white and sugar in a bowl until foamy. Whisk in the flour, melted butter and orange zest.

3 Put six dessertspoons of the mixture well apart on each of the prepared sheets. Spread each one to make an oval shape.

4 Bake one above the other in a preheated oven at 200°C/400°F/gas 6/fan oven 180°C for about 6 minutes until the biscuits are brown round the edges, swapping the sheets over half way through cooking.

5 Remove from the oven. Carefully lift off the sheet and transfer to a wire rack to cool completely. Store in an airtight container.

Walnut Cookies

Makes about 24

50 g/2 oz/¼ cup butter or margarine, plus extra for greasing
100 g/4 oz/½ cup light brown sugar
1 egg, beaten
25 g/1 oz/¼ cup walnut pieces, finely chopped
100 g/4 oz/1 cup plain (all-purpose) flour
1.5 ml/¼ tsp bicarbonate of soda (baking soda)

1 Beat the butter or margarine and sugar together in a bowl until light and fluffy.

2 Add the egg and walnuts and beat thoroughly.

3 Sift the flour and bicarbonate of soda over the surface and work in with a wooden spoon until the mixture forms a soft but not sticky dough. Knead gently on a lightly floured surface.

4 Shape into a thick sausage about 5 cm/2 in diameter and wrap in clingfilm (plastic wrap). Chill for several hours or overnight in the fridge.

5 Cut the sausage into 5mm/¼ in thick slices. Transfer to two lightly greased baking (cookie) sheets.

6 Place the baking sheets one above the other in a preheated oven at 180°C/350°F/gas 4/fan oven 160°C for about 10–12 minutes, swapping the sheets over half way through cooking.

7 Remove from the oven and transfer the cookies to a wire rack to cool completely. Store in an airtight container.

Chewy Treacle Drops

Makes about 15

100 g/4 oz/½ cup butter or margarine, softened, plus extra for greasing

1 egg

15 ml/1 tbsp black treacle (molasses)

15 ml/1 tbsp dark brown sugar

100 g/4 oz/1 cup Superfast Oats

50 g/2 oz/¼ cup caster (superfine) sugar

10 ml/2 tsp mixed (apple-pie) spice

1   Beat the butter or margarine, egg, treacle and brown sugar together until fluffy.

2   Work in the oats, caster sugar and spice.

3   Grease two baking (cookie) sheets. Drop heaped dessert-spoonfuls of the mixture on to the sheets and bake one above the other in a preheated oven at 180°C/350°F/gas 4/fan oven 160°C for 12–15 minutes until golden, swapping the sheets over half way through cooking. Don't overcook or they will become hard rather than chewy.

4   Remove from the oven and allow to cool slightly, then transfer to a wire rack to cool completely. Store in an airtight container.

Bumper Breakfast Bars

Packed with nutritious ingredients to give long-lasting energy, these bars are ideal when you have to skip breakfast or lunch. But don't just have them to replace a meal; they are ideal any time when you want a filling snack that's full of goodness.

Honeyed Cereal Bars

Makes 12

50 g/2 oz/¼ cup butter or margarine
100 g/4 oz/1 small packet of marshmallows
30 ml/2 tbsp clear honey
100 g/4 oz/2 cups crisped rice cereal
100 g/4 oz/1 cup Superfast Oats
100 g/2 oz/⅓ cup raisins
10 ml/2 tsp mixed (apple-pie) spice
Sunflower oil for greasing

1 Melt the butter or margarine, marshmallows and honey in a saucepan, stirring.
2 Stir in the rice cereal, oats, raisins and spice.
3 Press into an oiled 18 x 28 cm/7 x 11 in shallow baking tin (pan).
4 Leave to cool, then chill until firm. Cut into fingers. Store in an airtight container.

Apricot and Coconut Munch Bars

Makes 15

175 g/6 oz/1 small can of evaporated milk
20 ml/4 tsp thick honey
45 ml/3 tbsp apple juice
50 g/2 oz/¼ cup butter or hard block margarine, plus extra for greasing
50 g/2 oz/¼ cup light brown sugar
100 g/4 oz/⅔ cup sultanas (golden raisins)
225 g/8 oz/1⅓ cups dried apricots, chopped
100 g/4 oz/1 cup desiccated (shredded) coconut
225 g/8 oz/2 cups jumbo oats

1 Pour the evaporated milk into a saucepan and add the honey, apple juice, butter or margarine and sugar. Heat gently, stirring, until just melted. Remove from the heat.

2 Stir in the remaining ingredients until thoroughly blended.

3 Grease an 18 cm x 28 cm/7 in x 11 in shallow baking tin (pan). Press the mixture into the tin.

4 Wrap in clingfilm (plastic wrap) and chill for several hours or preferably overnight to allow the flavours to develop. Cut into bars and store in an airtight container in the fridge.

Banana Bonanza Bars

Makes 15

250 g/9 oz/2¼ cups Superfast Oats
75 g/3 oz/¾ cup desiccated (shredded) coconut
175 g/6 oz ready-to-eat prunes, stoned (pitted) and chopped
5 ml/1 tsp mixed (apple-pie) spice
75 g/3 oz/⅓ cup butter or margarine, plus extra for greasing
75 g/3 oz/⅓ cup light brown sugar
30 ml/2 tbsp clear honey
2 bananas
15 ml/1 tbsp lemon juice
100 g/4 oz/⅔ cup chopped cooking dates

1 Mix the oats with the coconut, prunes and spice.

2 Put the butter or margarine, sugar and honey in a saucepan and heat gently, stirring occasionally, until melted.

3 Add to the oat mixture and mix well.

4 Grease an 18 cm x 28 cm/7 in x 11 in shallow baking tin (pan). Press half the mixture in the tin.

5 Slice the bananas fairly thinly and mix with the lemon juice and dates. Spread over the oat mixture, then top with the remaining oat mixture and press down well.

6 Bake in a preheated oven at 180°C/350°F/gas 4/fan oven 160°C for 30 minutes until a rich golden brown.

7 Remove from the oven and allow to cool slightly, then mark into 15 bars. Allow to cool completely in the tin before cutting into bars. Store in an airtight container in the fridge.

Malted Muesli Bars

Makes 15

For the bars:
175 g/6 oz/1½ cups jumbo oats
A pinch of salt
50 g/2 oz/½ cup currants
25 g/1 oz/¼ cup chopped mixed nuts
25 g/1 oz/3 tbsp sultanas (golden raisins)
60 ml/4 tbsp malted milk drink powder
75 g/3 oz/⅓ cup butter or margarine, plus extra for greasing
45 ml/3 tbsp clear honey
For the topping:
100 g/4 oz/½ cup butter or margarine
100 g/4 oz/½ cup light brown sugar
15 ml/1 tbsp cocoa (unsweetened chocolate) powder
15 ml/1 tbsp milk

1 Make the bars. Mix the dry ingredients together in a bowl.

2 Put the butter or margarine and honey in a saucepan and heat gently, stirring, until melted. Pour into the dry ingredients and mix well. Don't bother to wash out the saucepan – you can use it for the topping.

3 Grease an 18 cm x 28 cm/7 in x 11 in shallow baking tin (pan). Press the mixture into the tin and bake in a preheated oven at 190°C/375°F/gas 5/fan oven 170°C for about 20 minutes until golden. Remove from the oven and leave to cool slightly while making the topping.

4 Put all the topping ingredients in the same saucepan. Heat gently until everything has melted. Cook, stirring, for 1 minute. Pour over the oat mixture, tipping the tin to help it spread and easing it into the corners with a knife. Leave until almost cold, then decorate the top with the prongs of a fork and cut into bars. Store in an airtight container.

Marmalade Pumpkin Bars

Makes 15

100 g/4 oz/1 cup wholemeal self-raising (self-rising) flour
150 g/5 oz/1¼ cups Superfast Oats
2.5 ml/½ tsp bicarbonate of soda (baking soda)
50 g/2 oz/½ cup pumpkin seeds
100 g/4 oz/½ cup butter or margarine, plus extra for greasing
100 g/4 oz/½ cup demerara sugar
15 ml/1 tbsp maple or golden (light corn) syrup
45 ml/3 tbsp orange shred marmalade

1   Mix the flour with 100 g/4 oz/1 cup of the oats, the bicarbonate of soda and the pumpkin seeds.

2   Put the butter or margarine, sugar and syrup in a saucepan and heat gently, stirring occasionally, until melted.

3   Stir in the oat mixture until thoroughly blended.

4   Grease an 18 cm x 28 cm/7 in x 11 in shallow baking tin (pan) and press the mixture into it. Spread the marmalade all over the top and sprinkle with the remaining oats.

5   Bake in a preheated oven at 180°C/350°F/gas 4/fan oven 160°C for 25 minutes.

6   Remove from the oven and allow to cool in the tin for 10 minutes, then cut into bars and transfer to a wire rack to cool completely. Store in an airtight container.

Strawberry Yoghurt and Raisin Breakfast Bars

These are also delicious made with lemon or vanilla yoghurt.

Makes 15

50 g/2 oz/½ cup jumbo oats
100 g/4 oz/1 cup plain (all-purpose) flour
75 g/3 oz/⅓ cup light brown sugar
1.5 ml/¼ tsp grated nutmeg
1.5 ml/¼ tsp ground cinnamon
150 g/5 oz/⅔ cup softened butter or soft tub margarine, plus extra for greasing
100 g/4 oz/2 cups bran flakes, crushed
250 ml/8 fl oz/1 cup strawberry yoghurt
1 egg, beaten
75 g/3 oz/½ cup raisins

1   Mix the oats with all but 30 ml/2 tbsp of the flour, the sugar and the spices in small bowl.

2   Add the butter or margarine and mash in with a fork. Work in the bran flakes.

3   Grease an 18 cm x 28 cm/7 in x 11 in a shallow baking tin (pan). Press half the mixture in the base of the tin.

4   Beat the yoghurt, egg and remaining flour together and stir in the raisins. Spread over the oat mixture in the tin, then sprinkle with the remaining oat mixture and press down lightly.

5   Bake in a preheated oven at 180°C/350°F/gas 4/fan oven 160°C for about 45 minutes or until golden brown.

6   Remove from the oven and allow to cool in the tin, then cut into bars. Store in an airtight container in the fridge.

Morning Apple Bars

These are so deliciously soft and moist, they make a fantastic dessert with custard too!

Makes 15

25 g/1 oz/¼ cup plain (all-purpose) flour
75 g/3 oz/¾ cup wholemeal flour
100 g/4 oz/1 cup Superfast Oats
2.5 ml/½ tsp salt
1.5 ml/¼ tsp bicarbonate of soda (baking soda)
1.5 ml/¼ tsp ground cloves
1.5 ml/¼ tsp mixed (apple-pie) spice
75 g/3 oz/⅓ cup demerara sugar
3 eating (dessert) apples, cored and grated, including the skin
10 ml/2 tsp lemon juice
1 egg, beaten
30 ml/2 tbsp sunflower oil
75 g/3 oz/½ cup sultanas (golden raisins)

1 Mix the flours, oats, salt, bicarbonate of soda, spices and demerara sugar together in a bowl.

2 Add all the remaining ingredients and mix well.

3 Grease an 18 cm x 28 cm/7 in x 11 in shallow baking tin (pan) and press the mixture into the tin.

4 Bake in a preheated oven at 180°C/350°F/gas 4/fan oven 160°C for about 35 minutes or until light golden brown and firm to the touch.

5 Remove from the oven and allow to cool in the tin, then cut into bars. Store in an airtight container in the fridge.

Chocolate Fruit and Peanut Bars

Makes 15

175 g/6 oz/³⁄₄ cup light brown sugar
75 ml/5 tbsp golden (light corn) syrup
40 g/1½ oz/3 tbsp butter or margarine, plus extra for greasing
90 ml/6 tbsp smooth peanut butter
100 g/4 oz/2 cups crisped rice cereal
75 g/3 oz/³⁄₄ cup jumbo oats
25 g/1 oz/¹⁄₄ cup wheat or oat bran
100 g/4 oz/1 cup chocolate chips
100 g/4 oz/²⁄₃ cup dried mixed fruit (fruit cake mix)

1 Put the sugar, syrup and butter or margarine in a large saucepan and heat gently until melted.

2 Remove from the heat and stir in the peanut butter until melted.

3 Add all the remaining ingredients and mix well.

4 Grease an 18 cm x 28 cm/7 in x 11 in shallow baking tin (pan). Press the mixture into the tin. Cool, then chill until firm. Cut into bars and store in an airtight container.

Savoury Specials

Biscuits don't have to be sweet. Here you'll find biscuits for cheese, great snacks that are kind to the teeth and tasty treats for breakfast with honey, jam or Marmite. In fact, all these savoury specials are ideal for nibbling at any time.

Parmesan Wafers

Makes 12

Oil for greasing
100 g/4 oz/1 cup freshly grated Parmesan cheese

1   Oil a baking (cookie) sheet. Put 12 spoonfuls of Parmesan cheese in small piles a little apart on the sheet. Flatten.

2   Bake in a preheated oven at 200°C/400°F/gas 6/fan oven 180°C for 10 minutes until melted.

3   Remove from the oven and leave to cool and become crisp. Store in an airtight container in the fridge.

Crispy Coarse Oatcakes

Makes 8

75 g/3 oz/¾ cup medium oatmeal, plus extra for dusting
A good pinch of salt
1.5 ml/¼ tsp bicarbonate of soda (baking soda)
15 g/½ oz/1 tbsp butter, melted
60 ml/4 tbsp hand-hot water
Oil for greasing

1 Mix all the ingredients except the oil together in a bowl until the mixture forms a dough.

2 Dust a surface with a little oatmeal, then turn out the dough on to it. Roll out thinly to a large round, about 25 cm/10 in diameter, using a saucepan lid or dinner plate as a guide.

3 Cut into 8 wedges.

4 Lightly grease a large heavy-based frying pan (skillet) and cook the oatcakes, four at a time, for about 3 minutes until firm. Carefully turn them over and cook for a further 2 minutes until crisp. Cool on a wire rack. Re-grease the pan before cooking the second batch.

5 When cold, store in an airtight container.

Baked Fine Oatcakes

Makes 16

225 g/8 oz/2 cups fine oatmeal
A pinch of salt
A pinch of bicarbonate of soda (baking soda)
40 g/1½ oz/3 tbsp lard or white vegetable fat (shortening), melted
45 ml/3 tbsp hot water
45 ml/3 tbsp cold milk
Oil for greasing

1 Mix the oatmeal, salt and bicarbonate of soda together in a bowl.

2 Add the lard or vegetable fat, the water and milk and mix to form a soft but not sticky dough. Knead lightly, then cut in half and roll out each half to a round about 20 cm/8 in diameter, using a saucepan lid or plate as a guide.

3 Cut each round into eight wedges.

4 Lightly oil a baking (cookie) sheet. Place the wedges on the sheet and bake in a preheated oven at 180°C/350°F/gas 4/ fan oven 160°C for 25–30 minutes until golden brown and curling at the edges.

5 Remove from the oven and transfer to a wire rack to cool. Store in an airtight container.

Savoury Crackers

These are nice on their own, with cheese or spread with a savoury spread for a snack meal.

Makes about 18
75 g/3 oz/¾ cup wholemeal flour
100 g/4 oz/1 cup plain (all-purpose) flour, plus extra for dusting
25 g/1 oz/¼ cup oat bran
2.5 ml/½ tsp onion or celery salt
5 ml/1 tsp bicarbonate of soda (baking soda)
150 g/5 oz/⅔ cup butter or margarine, plus extra for greasing
A little water

1 Mix the flours, bran, flavoured salt and bicarbonate of soda in a bowl. Work in the butter or margarine with a fork.

2 Add water, if necessary, a drop at a time to form a soft but not sticky dough.

3 Knead gently on a lightly floured surface. Roll out thinly to a rectangle, then cut into 5 cm/2 in squares. Transfer to a lightly greased baking (cookie) sheet.

4 Bake in a preheated oven at 180°C/350°F/gas 4/fan oven 160°C for about 30 minutes until lightly browned.

5 Remove from the oven and allow to cool slightly, then transfer to a wire rack to cool completely. Store in an airtight container.

Cheese and Poppy Seed Straws

Makes about 48

100 g/4 oz/1 cup plain (all-purpose) flour, plus extra for dusting
A good pinch each of salt, white pepper and cayenne
65 g/2½ oz/scant ⅓ cup butter, cut into small pieces,
plus extra for greasing
65 g/2½ oz/scant ¾ cup finely grated Cheddar cheese
1 egg, separated
15 ml/1 tbsp poppy seeds

1   Sift together the flour, salt, pepper and cayenne.

2   Add the butter and rub in using the fingertips. Stir in the cheese.

3   Mix in the egg yolk, adding 1–2 tsp of the egg white so the mixture forms a stiff dough.

4   Knead gently on a lightly floured surface. Roll out to a rectangle about 5 mm/¼ in thick, then cut into strips about 7.5 cm/3 in wide. Brush the strips with lightly beaten egg white, then sprinkle with the poppy seeds. Cut the strips into narrow fingers and transfer to a greased baking (cookie) sheet.

5   Bake in a preheated oven at 180°C/350°F/gas 4/fan oven 160°C for about 7 minutes until lightly golden.

6   Remove from the oven and allow to cool slightly, then transfer to a wire rack to cool completely. Store in an airtight container.

Cheese and Nut Cookies

Makes about 12

75 g/3 oz/⅓ cup butter, plus extra for greasing
50 g/2 oz/½ cup finely grated Red Leicester cheese
75 g/3 oz/¾ cup self-raising (self-rising) flour
25 g/1 oz/¼ cup fine oatmeal
A good pinch each of salt and pepper
2.5 ml/½ tsp paprika
40 g/1½ oz/⅓ cup chopped mixed nuts
Whole blanched almonds, to decorate

1 Beat the butter with the cheese until blended, then work in the flour, oatmeal, salt, pepper, paprika and chopped nuts.

2 Shape the mixture into small balls with lightly floured hands.

3 Place the balls well apart on a greased baking (cookie) sheet. Press an almond into the top of each.

4 Bake in a preheated oven at 160°C/325°F/gas 3/fan oven 145°C for about 15 minutes until pale golden brown.

5 Remove from the oven and allow to cool for 10 minutes, then transfer to a wire rack to cool completely. Store in an airtight container.

Caraway Biscuits

Makes about 32

225 g/8 oz/2 cups plain (all-purpose) flour,
plus extra for dusting

1.5 ml/¼ tsp salt

50 g/2 oz/¼ cup butter or margarine, cut into small pieces,
plus extra for greasing

15 g/½ oz/1 tbsp caster (superfine) sugar

5 ml/1 tsp caraway seeds

1 large egg, beaten

About 30 ml/2 tbsp milk

1 Mix the flour and salt in a bowl. Add the butter or margarine and rub in using the fingertips.

2 Stir in the sugar and seeds.

3 Mix with the beaten egg and enough of the milk to form a firm dough.

4 Knead gently on a lightly floured surface. Roll out thinly and cut into 5 cm/2 in squares.

5 Transfer to two greased baking (cookie) sheets. Bake one above the other in a preheated oven at 180°C/350°F/ gas 4/fan oven 160°C for about 15 minutes until a pale biscuit colour, swapping the sheets over half way through cooking.

6 Remove from the oven and allow to cool slightly, then transfer to a wire rack to cool completely. Store in an airtight container.

Digestive Biscuits

These biscuits are so melting they break very easily, so handle them gently!

Makes about 12

50 g/2 oz/½ cup wholemeal flour

50 g/2 oz/½ cup plain (all-purpose) flour, plus extra for dusting

100 g/4 oz/1 cup medium oatmeal

15 g/½ oz/1 tbsp caster (superfine) sugar

1.5 ml/¼ tsp salt

1.5 ml/¼ tsp bicarbonate of soda (baking soda)

100 g/4 oz/½ cup butter or margarine, cut into small pieces, plus extra for greasing

A little milk, to mix

1   Mix all the dry ingredients thoroughly together in a bowl.

2   Rub in the butter or margarine and mix, adding 5 ml/1 tsp of milk at a time, to form a soft but not sticky dough.

3   Roll out thinly on a lightly floured surface. Cut into rounds using a 7.5 cm/3 in cutter.

4   Arrange on two greased baking (cookie) sheets. Bake one above the other in a preheated oven at 200°C/400°F/gas 6/fan oven 180°C for 7–8 minutes until golden brown, swapping the sheets over half way through cooking.

5   Remove from the oven and allow to cool slightly, then transfer to a wire rack to cool completely. Store in an airtight container.

Caribbean Fried Biscuits

These are particularly delicious with cheese.

Makes 12

225 g/8 oz/2 cups self-raising (self-rising) flour,
plus extra for dusting

15 g/½ oz/2 tbsp oat bran

5 ml/1 tsp salt

25 g/1 oz/2 tbsp white vegetable fat (shortening),
cut into small pieces

10 ml/2 tsp caster (superfine) sugar

About 60 ml/4 tbsp water

Oil for shallow-frying

1   Mix the flour, oat bran and salt in a bowl. Add the fat and rub in using the fingertips until the mixture resembles fine breadcrumbs.

2   Stir in the sugar, then mix with enough of the water to form a firm dough, adding a little extra water if necessary.

3   Knead gently on a lightly floured surface.

4   Divide the mixture into 12 small balls, then roll out each piece to a round about 5 mm/¼ in thick.

5   Heat about 5 mm/¼ in oil in a large frying pan (skillet). Fry the biscuits a few at a time for 3–4 minutes on each side, reducing the heat if browning too quickly, until cooked through and a rich golden brown and crisp on the outside.

6   Drain on kitchen paper (paper towels) and serve warm or just cooled.

No-bake Cookies

Apart from having to melt a few ingredients, none of these needs any baking whatsoever. This makes them especially good for children to make, being simple and quick to prepare. The only boring part is you have to wait for them to set before tucking in!

Walnut Fudge Fingers

If you don't like nuts, substitute raisins instead.

Makes 15

175 g/6 oz plain rich tea biscuits

3 small chocolate fudge finger bars

100 g/4 oz/½ cup butter or margarine, plus extra for greasing

175 g/6 oz/1 cup icing (confectioners') sugar,
plus extra for dusting

15 ml/1 tbsp cocoa (unsweetened chocolate) powder

15 ml/1 tbsp milk

15 ml/1 tbsp lemon juice

50 g/2 oz/½ cup walnut pieces, roughly chopped

1   Put the biscuits in a plastic bag and roughly crush with a rolling pin.

2   Break up the fudge bars and place them in a saucepan.

3   Add the butter or margarine, icing sugar, cocoa, milk and lemon juice. Heat gently, stirring all the time, until melted.

4   Stir in the crushed biscuits and nuts.

5   Grease an 18 cm/7 in square shallow baking tin (pan) and press the biscuit mixture into the tin. Cool, then chill until firm. Dust with icing sugar and cut into fingers. Store in an airtight container.

Chocolate Nut and Apricot Bars

Makes 12–16

175 g/6 oz/³⁄₄ cup butter or hard block margarine,
plus extra for greasing
50 g/2 oz/¹⁄₄ cup light brown sugar
30 ml/2 tbsp golden (light corn) syrup
45 ml/3 tbsp cocoa (unsweetened chocolate) powder
100 g/4 oz/²⁄₃ cup ready-to-eat dried apricots, chopped
250 g/9 oz/2¹⁄₄ cups jumbo oats
75 g/3 oz/³⁄₄ cup chopped mixed nuts
200 g/7 oz/1³⁄₄ cups plain (semi-sweet) cooking chocolate,
chopped

1 Grease an 18 cm x 28 cm/7 in x 11 in shallow baking tin (pan) and line with non-stick baking parchment.

2 Put the butter or margarine in a saucepan with the sugar, syrup and cocoa. Heat gently, stirring, until melted. Stir in the apricots, oats and nuts.

3 Press into the prepared tin.

4 Melt the chocolate in a bowl over a pan of hot water. Alternatively, melt the chocolate briefly in the microwave. Spread over the surface of the oat mixture, right to the corners. Chill until set.

5 Cut into fingers and store in an airtight container.

Chocolate Minted Mallow Sandwiches

Makes 9

50 g/2 oz/¹/₄ cup butter or margarine, plus extra for greasing
45 ml/3 tbsp golden (light corn) syrup
50 g/2 oz/¹/₄ cup caster (superfine) sugar
100 g/4 oz/1 cup plain (semi-sweet) chocolate, chopped
100 g/4 oz/2 cups crisped rice cereal
15 g/¹/₂ oz/2 tbsp oat bran
200 g/7 oz/1 packet of small white marshmallows
A few drops of peppermint essence (extract)

1   Put the butter or margarine, syrup and sugar in a pan and heat gently, stirring occasionally, until melted.

2   Remove from the heat and stir in the chocolate until melted. Mix in the rice cereal and bran.

3   Grease an 18 cm/7 in square shallow baking tin (pan) and press half the mixture into the tin.

4   Quickly melt the marshmallows in a saucepan, stirring all the time, then add a few drops of peppermint essence to taste.

5   Quickly spread the mallow over the chocolate mixture. Cover with the remaining chocolate rice mixture and press down gently. Cool, chill until firm, then cut into squares. Store in an airtight container.

Triple Layer Bites

These need to be cut quite small as they are very rich!

Makes 20

For the base layer:

150 g/5 oz/²⁄₃ cup butter or hard block margarine,
plus extra for greasing

250 g/9 oz/1 small packet of plain digestive biscuits
(graham crackers)

40 g/1½ oz/3 tbsp light brown sugar

45 ml/3 tbsp cocoa (unsweetened chocolate) powder

5 ml/1 tsp instant coffee granules

1 egg, beaten

5 ml/1 tsp vanilla essence (extract)

50 g/2 oz/½ cup desiccated (shredded) coconut

50 g/2 oz/½ cup finely chopped brazil nuts

For the middle layer:

30 ml/2 tbsp custard powder

50 g/2 oz/¼ cup softened butter or soft tub margarine

225 g/8 oz/1⅓ cups icing (confectioners') sugar

30 ml/2 tbsp boiling water

For the top layer:

50 g/2 oz/¼ cup butter or margarine

150 g/5 oz/1¼ cups plain (semi-sweet) chocolate

75 g/3 oz/½ cup icing sugar

1   Make the base layer. Grease an 18 cm x 28 cm/7 in x 11 in shallow baking tin (pan). Put the biscuits in a bag and crush finely with a rolling pin.

2   Put the butter, margarine, sugar, cocoa and coffee in a saucepan and heat gently, stirring occasionally, until melted.

3   Whisk in the egg and vanilla and continue to heat, stirring for 1 minute, but do not boil.

4   Stir in the crushed biscuits, the coconut and brazil nuts until

well mixed, then press it into the prepared tin. Chill while making the next layer.

5 Beat all the middle layer ingredients together until thoroughly blended. Spread over the biscuit layer and chill for at least 30 minutes.

6 Meanwhile, make the top layer. Put the butter or margarine in a bowl. Break up the chocolate and add it to the bowl. Place the bowl over a pan of hot water and stir until the chocolate melts. Alternatively, melt briefly in the microwave.

7 Sift the icing sugar over the surface and work in until smooth. Spread over the custard layer and chill until firm. Cut into small squares. Store in an airtight container.

Honey and Peanut Squares

Makes 9

75 g/3 oz/⅓ cup butter or hard block margarine,
plus extra for greasing
200 g/7 oz plain broken biscuits
45 ml/3 tbsp thick honey
5 ml/1 tsp finely grated lemon zest
45 ml/3 tbsp crunchy peanut butter
25 g/1 oz/¼ cup wheat or oat bran

1 Put the butter or margarine in a saucepan and heat until melted, stirring occasionally. Bring to the boil.

2 Meanwhile, crush the biscuits in a bag with a rolling pin.

3 Stir the honey, lemon zest and peanut butter into the pan, then add the biscuits and bran and mix thoroughly.

4 Grease an 18 cm/7 in square shallow baking tin (pan) and press the mixture into the tin. Leave until cold, then chill until firm. Cut into squares and store in an airtight container.

Cranberry Crunch Squares

Makes 9

75 g/3 oz/⅓ cup butter or margarine, plus extra for greasing
60 ml/4 tbsp clear honey
50 g/2 oz/¼ cup caster (superfine) sugar
100 g/4 oz/2 cups cornflakes, crushed
50 g/2 oz/½ cup jumbo oats
75 g/3 oz/½ cup dried cranberries
100 g/4 oz/1 cup white chocolate

1 Put the butter or margarine, honey and sugar in a saucepan and heat gently, stirring occasionally, until melted. Boil for 1 minute.

2 Stir in the cornflakes, oats and cranberries until well blended.

3 Grease an 18 cm/7 in square shallow baking tin (pan). Spoon the mixture into the tin and press down well.

4 Break up the chocolate and melt in a bowl over a pan of hot water. Alternatively, melt the chocolate briefly in the microwave. Spread over the mixture in the tin, then chill until firm. Cut into squares and store in an airtight container in the fridge.

Chocolate Sultana Slabs

You can buy broken biscuits very cheaply, which are ideal for this recipe.

Makes 15

225 g/8 oz/2 cups plain biscuits

100 g/4 oz/½ cup butter or margarine, plus extra for greasing

15 g/½ oz/1 tbsp caster (superfine) sugar

15 ml/1 tbsp golden (light corn) syrup

30 ml/2 tbsp cocoa (unsweetened chocolate) powder

50 g/2 oz/⅓ cup sultanas (golden raisins)

1 Put the biscuits in a bag and roughly crush with a rolling pin.

2 Put the butter or margarine, sugar, syrup and cocoa in a pan and heat gently, stirring occasionally, until melted and well blended. Do not boil.

3 Stir in the biscuits and sultanas.

4 Grease an 18 cm x 28 cm/7 in x 11 in shallow baking tin (pan). Press the mixture into the tin, then chill until firm. Cut into fingers and store in an airtight container.

Cherry and Date Cookies

Makes about 12

50 g/2 oz/¼ cup butter or margarine

45 ml/3 tbsp golden (light corn) syrup

50 g/2 oz/¼ cup caster (superfine) sugar

100 g/4 oz/1 cup Superfast Oats

Oil for greasing

50 g/2 oz/¼ cup glacé (candied) cherries, chopped

100 g/4 oz/⅔ cup chopped cooking dates

1 Melt the butter or margarine with the syrup and sugar in a saucepan, stirring occasionally.

2 Stir in the oats and press half in a lightly oiled 18 cm/7 in square shallow baking tin (pan).

3 Mix the cherries and dates together and spread over the oat mixture in the tin. Top with the remaining oat mixture and press down firmly. Chill until firm, then cut into fingers. Store in an airtight container.

Double Chocolate Bites

Makes about 15

100 g/4 oz shortcake biscuits, crushed but not too finely
100 g/4 oz/²⁄₃ cup raisins
175 g/6 oz/1½ cups white chocolate, broken into pieces
175 g/6 oz/1½ cups plain (semi-sweet) chocolate,
broken into pieces
75 g/3 oz/⅓ cup butter

1 Mix the biscuits with the raisins. Chop half the white chocolate and add.

2 Melt the dark chocolate and the butter in a bowl over a pan of hot water. Alternatively, melt briefly in the microwave. Stir until smooth and blended, then stir into the biscuit mixture.

3 Spoon half the mixture on to each of two sheets of greaseproof (waxed) paper or non-stick baking parchment. Shape each into a sausage about 15 cm/6 in long and wrap securely. Chill in the fridge until firm.

4 Melt the remaining white chocolate in a bowl over a pan of hot water or melt briefly in the microwave.

5 Cut the chocolate sausage into slices about 1 cm/½ in thick and lay on the other side of the greaseproof paper or baking parchment. Using a teaspoon, trickle the white chocolate in a spiral pattern on top of each slice and leave to set. Store in an airtight container in the fridge.

Index

almonds
  almond macaroons 55
  almond tuiles 16–17
  apricot almond jammies 42–43
  biscotti 20–21
  fig and almond slices 27
apples
  date and apple squares 30
  morning apple bars 73
apricots
  apricot almond jammies 42–43
  apricot and coconut munch bars 68
  chocolate nut and apricot bars 86

baked fine oatcakes 77
banana bonanza bars 69
bars
  apricot and coconut munch bars 68
  banana bonanza bars 69
  chocolate fruit and peanut bars 7
  chocolate nut and apricot bars 86
  honeyed cereal bars 67
  malted muesli bars 70
  marmalade pumpkin bars 71
  moreish mallow bars 63
  morning apple bars 73
  strawberry yoghurt and raisin
    breakfast bars 72
biscotti 20–21
black and white Florentines 22–23
blueberry melts 59
Bourbon creams 47
bran 4
brandy snaps 19
brownies
  chocolate pecan brownies 28–29
  sticky ginger nut brownies 32–33
butter oat fingers 16
butter shorties 56–57

caramel
  chocolate caramel squares 61
caraway biscuits 81
Caribbean fried biscuits 83

cheese
  cheese and nut cookies 80
  cheese and poppy seed straws 79
  Parmesan wafers 75
cherries
  cherry and date cookies 92
  cherry and sultana slices 62
  cherry streusels 33
chewy treacle drops 66
chocolate
  black and white Florentines 22–23
  Bourbon creams 47
  chocolate caramel squares 61
  chocolate fruit and peanut bars 74
  chocolate jumbles 57
  chocolate kisses 45
  chocolate minted mallow
    sandwiches 87
  chocolate nut and apricot bars 86
  chocolate pecan brownies 28–29
  chocolate sultana slabs 91
  cranberry crunch squares 90
  double chocolate bites 93
  double chocolate crisps 14–15
  galas 40
  hazelnut chocolate chip
    shortbread 50
  honey pistachio chocolate dips 46
  triple layer bites 88–89
  walnut fudge fingers 85
coconut
  apricot and coconut munch bars 68
  coconut oat cookies 21
coffee
  coffee and walnut meringue
    tops 34–35
  coffee treats 39
cookies
  cherry and date cookies 92
  coconut oat cookies 21
  pine nut cinnamon cookies 31
  stem ginger and orange cookies 25
  sunflower vanilla cookies 13
  walnut cookies 65

Cornish fairings 17
crackers, savoury 78
cranberry crunch squares 90
cream buttons 51
crisped rice cereal
    toffee squares 60
crispy coarse oatcakes 76
custard creams 48

dates
    cherry and date cookies 92
    date and apple squares 30
digestive biscuits 82
double chocolate bites 93
double chocolate crisps 14–15

fig and almond slices 27
flapjacks
    fruity flapjacks 62–63
Florentines
    black and white Florentines 22–23
fruity flapjacks 62–63

galas 40
Garibaldi biscuits, iced 44–45
ginger
    stem ginger and orange cookies 25
    sticky ginger nut brownies 32–33

hazelnuts
    biscotti 20–21
    hazelnut chocolate chip
        shortbread 50
honey
    honey and peanut squares 89
    honey pistachio chocolate dips 46
    honeyed cereal bars 67

iced and sandwich biscuits
    apricot almond jammies 42–43
    Bourbon creams 47
    chocolate kisses 45
    chocolate nut and apricot bars 86
    coffee treats 39
    cranberry crunch squares 90
    custard creams 48
    double chocolate bites 93
    galas 40
    honey pistachio chocolate dips 46
    iced Garibaldi biscuits 44–45
    jammy sangers 43

lime or lemon tops 41
orange oat trickles 37
vanilla ices 38
Viennese fingers 53

jam
    apricot almond jammies 42–43
    jammy sangers 43

lemons
    lemon thins 56
    lime or lemon tops 41

macaroons
    almond macaroons 55
malted muesli bars 70
marmalade pumpkin bars 71
marshmallows
    chocolate minted mallow
        sandwiches 87
    moreish mallow bars 63
    toffee squares 60
meringues
    coffee and walnut meringue
        tops 34–35
    spiced toasted oat and cherry
        meringues 54–55
moreish mallow bars 63
Mornflake 5
morning apple bars 73
muesli 7
    malted muesli bars 70

nuts
    cheese and nut cookies 80
    chocolate nut and apricot bars 86
    see also individual types

oat crunchies 18
oat thins 15
oatcakes
    baked fine oatcakes 77
    crispy coarse oatcakes 76
oats 4, 5
    history 6–7
    milling 9–10
    types of 7–8
oranges
    orange drops 64
    orange oat trickles 37

palmiers 58
Parmesan wafers 75
pastries
    cheese and poppy seed straws 79
    palmiers 58
peanuts
    chocolate fruit and peanut bars 74
    honey and peanut squares 89
    peanut and oat crispies 24
pecans
    chocolate pecan brownies 28–29
petticoat oat tails 49
pine nut cinnamon cookies 31
pistachios
    honey pistachio chocolate dips 46
plain dunkers 23
poppy seeds
    cheese and poppy seed straws 79
pumpkin seeds
    marmalade pumpkin bars 71

raspberry oat squares 29

savoury biscuits
    baked fine oatcakes 77
    caraway biscuits 81
    Caribbean fried biscuits 83
    cheese and nut cookies 80
    cheese and poppy seed straws 79
    crispy coarse oatcakes 76
    digestive biscuits 82
    Parmesan wafers 75
    savoury crackers 78

shortbread
    hazelnut chocolate chip
        shortbread 50
    petticoat oat tails 49
spiced toasted oat and cherry
        meringues 54–55
stem ginger and orange cookies 25
sticky ginger nut brownies 32–33
strawberry yoghurt and raisin
        breakfast bars 72
sunflower vanilla cookies 13

toffee squares 60
treacle
    chewy treacle drops 66
triple layer bites 88–89

vanilla ices 38
Viennese fingers 53
Viennese whirls 52

walnuts
    coffee and walnut meringue
        tops 34–35
    sticky ginger nut brownies 32–33
    walnut cookies 65
    walnut fudge fingers 85

yoghurt
    strawberry yoghurt and raisin
        breakfast bars 72